PRODUCTIVITY
FOR
INFPs

HOW TO BE PRODUCTIVE WITHIN YOUR NATURAL RHYTHMS

AMANDA LINEHAN

PRODUCTIVITY FOR INFPS
How To Be Productive Within Your Natural Rhythms

Copyright © 2020 by Amanda Linehan

ISBN: 9798615349768

Cover art by Amanda Linehan
Interior design by Amanda Linehan

www.amandalinehan.com

Give feedback on the book at:
amanda@amandalinehan.com

Twitter: @amandalinehan

First Edition

Create and share.

INTRODUCTION

Hi, I'm Amanda and I'm an INFP.

If you're reading this book you likely already know what those letters mean and that you are one too (or maybe you're very close, like an INFJ), but either way I won't do any explaining about what an INFP is or any of the functions or any of that. This book is about how to get stuff done in a way that is aligned with your personality and preferences.

I first had the idea for this book a few months ago when I realized that many of the blog posts I had written over the last eleven years were about productivity in some way. However, they weren't just about productivity, they were about productivity the INFP-way, which is definitely different than your average person. Nothing wrong with the average person, by the way, we just tend to do things a little differently.

I've been blogging at amandalinehan.com since 2008 (!) and I've written about many different subjects, but issues around productivity kept cropping up.

You see, I've spent so much time thinking about my own productivity and the best way for me to get things done, I would often share it on my blog. I knew that many of the traditional productivity methods just didn't work that well for me. I use a calendar, but in a very loose way. I don't use any written to-do lists. I don't like to be scheduled tightly and I prefer to use my intuition when it comes to picking tasks to do rather than analytical decision making. But I had to figure out how best to make these things work for me because when it came to advice and recommendations I'd see the same stuff over and over that didn't work that well for me.

Hence, this book.

All of the sections of this book are made up of posts from my blog, but I've compiled and organized them into something that is easy to read and all in one place. On my website, they are scattered around from year to year and not always labeled that well in terms of tags and categories (something to work on!) so you actually know what you're looking at. I figured it was time to get this stuff all in one place.

If there's one thing that I would say characterizes the IN-FP's productivity needs, its SPACE. The space to use your intuition. The space to not feel too pressured (we're generally not great under lots of deadlines or schedules). The space to allow ideas and inspiration to float up into our minds. The space to play. The space to meander while we work. The space to work in a circular fashion, not in a linear one. The space to create.

Because that is one thing we love to do—create. INFPs may have odd working habits, but as a general rule we are very creative. Lots of artists and writers in this group. And we may be more driven and ambitious than people realize. Maybe even ourselves. There is a lot we want to put out into the world.

But we can also get overwhelmed very quickly. Traditional productivity methods may very well leave us more stressed than when we began them. And lots of stress doesn't help us create.

So, the ideas in this book are all to help you craft a productivity plan (sounds very practical doesn't it!)that actually works for you, instead of making you feel crazy.

And now a little bit more about me:

I'm an indie (self-published) fiction author and have been since 2012 (full time since 2017). I have published five novels—three young adult, one adult fiction, and one adult urban fantasy (vampires!). I've also published six short stories and two short story collections. You can check out all of my fiction at amandalinehan.com/fiction. I have two short stories published by someone other than me—one in an anthology and one in an online magazine and I send a newsletter each month with a free short story inside. That's a lot of stories that I've written and published in one way or another. So that's pretty productive.

At my old job—I worked in research grant administration—I was promoted three times and even won an award in the ten years I was there. The point isn't to brag, it's just to say that I've been able to figure out how to be productive at my current career and in my old one too. But, it took a lot of trial and error. :)

So, I invite you to take a look at the ideas in this book and begin trying what seems like it might be a good fit for you. They might not all work, but I'm confident you will take away at least a few pieces that will help you get your creations out into the world.

Because the world needs you to create and share.

Feel free to send me an email at amanda@amandalinehan. com if you have a question, or feedback or just want to say hi. I love hearing from fellow INFPs and those who are interested in personality.

PART ONE:

STARTING AND MOVING FORWARD

Where To Start

You know that you want to get somewhere, or at least you know that you need to start walking. But, where to start?

Well, the easiest place to start is by putting one foot in front of the other. Simple.

But what if that foot doesn't seem to want to move? How do you get started when you feel more like a block of ice than a meandering stream?

Take The Absolute Smallest Step You Can Take

This still moves you forward (you only want to go backwards if that also takes you forward) and is very manageable when you are looking at a long road ahead.

Also, when you are taking the smallest step forward you don't need a "lion-amount" of courage, you may just need a "house cat-amount" of courage. (Then, as you continue to take more steps you can develop your lion-amount of courage.)

What's really important is to move forward, even if it's only a centimeter (or a millimeter!).

But, what if you are really unsure of even the smallest step ahead?

Consider That You Already Know What The First Step Is

Maybe you just don't want to do it, or feel that you don't have quite enough courage yet. Or maybe you anticipate that it will be uncomfortable.

Use your intuition to confirm what that first step needs to be and trust that you will be able to handle what comes after that first step.

Getting started is not really about knowing what to do first, but knowing that you have the ability to do what needs to come first.

So take that first (tiny) step.

What Can I Do?

The next time you are feeling stuck, ask yourself the following question:

What can I do?

This is opposed to thinking about all of the things you can't do or don't have control over in any given situation. That is probably a very long list, but the things you can do is a shorter list and, therefore, easier to focus on.

When you ask what you can do, you stop trying to control the world around you, and you simply focus on yourself. You take responsibility for the things you can be responsible for and you leave the rest up to life.

This is certainly a much more peaceful approach to living than trying to control everything. You will definitely fail at that.

Once you have your list, start taking action (or non-action as it may be). The simple act of being responsible for the things that you have the ability to be responsible for will automatically create change in your life because you will begin to feel more powerful.

Not powerful in a rule-the-world kind of way, but personally powerful. The power to create change in your life, the power to improve your life and the power to accept things you can't change.

Just as you are responsible for your stuff, other people are responsible for their stuff.

And, if you take care of your stuff, you can let other people take care of theirs.

The Skill of Figuring It Out

Sometimes you don't know what you're doing, you don't have everything you need and you feel stuck. In this instance you need to employ the skill of figuring-it-out.

Figuring-it-out is a useful skill to have, but one that takes practice to develop. It's handy in any situation where you feel overwhelmed and haven't got a clue how to proceed.

Figuring-it-out encompasses any skill/talent/accident that takes you a step closer to what you need/want to achieve. It's always there with you when you call on it, and is a toolbox filled with an infinite number of tools of infinite variety.

In the midst of figuring-it-out you often feel even worse than when you started. That's because you've put yourself in the midst of whatever mess it is that you are dealing with. It feels uncomfortable, but really things are getting better, because you have the courage to face whatever it is head on.

Figuring-it-out is really a collection of tiny steps and small tools, which taken together, creates more than the sum of its parts. Soon enough, you will have taken so many tiny steps with small tools that you actually begin to get somewhere, even if it feels like you've been stumbling around from place to place. If stumbling is the only way you can get somewhere, I'd take it. It's usually better than standing still.

The great thing about figuring-it-out, is that at the end when you look back, you may still have no idea how you actually got to where you did. It may feel like a jumble of accidents, timely help and a few small skills you possess that you had no idea would make any difference. But you made it anyway and you did it with whatever you had at the time and any help that came along the way. And really, that's what figuring-it-out is all about.

If you knew exactly what you were going to do and how it was going to get done, it wouldn't be figuring-it-out. That would be a plan, which is nice to have, but often in the most difficult circumstances we have no plan.

But luckily for you, you have figuring-it-out.

Focus On The Process, Not The Results

When I have a goal or I want something, I tend to get really caught up in the results that I'm looking for.

But what I've learned is that it's better to focus on the process of what you're doing, and let the results flow from there.

When I focus on results, I tend to tighten up creatively, because I'm attached to something particular happening. I miss good things along the way that might have helped me get to where I want to go, because they don't seem to support the thing that I want.

I also miss out on a bit of adventure, because I'm trying too hard to hang on to certainty.

When I'm focused on the process of what I'm doing, I see things on the periphery that seem like they might be good to follow, so I do, and it usually turns out pretty well.

Also, I just enjoy myself more because I can let go of the anxiety I feel when I'm attached to a certain result. The path in front of me is richer because I can consider a detour at any time.

Take blogging, for instance. You can fret and worry about the traffic and subscriptions you are (or aren't) getting, or you can focus on all the small pieces it takes to keep up a successful blog with a readership – posting consistently, creating the best content you can, responding to your readers, guest posting, sharing your content on social media (appropriately!), etc.

There is a lot you don't control, but there are a few things that you do, so focus on doing those, and leave the rest up to the life.

If you have a blog and do all those things above, in some time you will have a blog with a nice, steady readership, and maybe one day you'll have wild success.

But I wouldn't worry about that too much now, just do the little things. It'll add up.

Going With The Flow Of Your Energy

It's happened to me so many times.

It's the middle of the afternoon and I'm trying to work on something, but I'm not getting anywhere. I keep hitting dead ends of various sorts and I'm getting a little frustrated. Then I decide to put the work aside and come back to it the next morning, maybe.

And voila! Suddenly everything is falling into place. Things that confused me the day before are no longer confusing. Problems that seemed unsolvable are solving themselves. And it's not the result of magic.

It's the result of me working with my energy rather than against it.

I'm a morning person. I have the most energy before lunchtime. And I try to keep that in mind as I work on stuff—making sure my most energy-consuming activities happen in the morning.

But every once in a while, for whatever reason, I try to get something done in the middle of the afternoon that takes too much energy. At 3pm I'm a little sluggish. I can handle smaller tasks or things that don't require a lot of brain power, but if I really need to be at peak creativity, I shouldn't be working on it then if at all possible.

For instance, yesterday afternoon I was working on a book cover and as I played around with different elements nothing quite seemed to be coming together and I got a little frustrated. I didn't go back to it this morning but I realized that it was probably a better morning activity, and that my frustration might have been coming from resisting my energy rather than the fact that nothing is working.

My prediction is that the next time I work on that in the morning, things will be fine and will seem to come together much easier than yesterday. Instead of forcing my way through that activity, I'll wait for the right time to work on it. It'll all come together.

Curiosity

The next time curiosity grabs you and wants to take you somewhere, go wherever it wants you to go. Even if wherever it's leading you seems odd or unnecessary or if it seems to have no purpose for your life.

In fact, curiosity is often the most rewarding if it seems to have no purpose for your life.

Maybe the best thing about curiosity is that it "forces" you to be playful. If you are following your whims and not looking for any results there's nothing left to do but play with whatever makes you curious. And whatever you get out of it is simply a gift, something that you weren't expecting.

Curiosity operates outside of your plans. You can't plan to be curious. That's why it's so fun. You're driving along a fast, straight highway just trying to get where you're going, and curiosity is the billboard that catches your eye and makes you want to stop and explore.

It might slow you down and it might not help you get where you're going, but it sure is fun and interesting. And, you know, you can always get back in your car when you're done and continue on.

How To Solve Any Problem

The simplest way to tackle any problem:

Always Go Forward

Even the tiniest motion forward is better than standing still (or going backward – although you can actually go backwards to move forward). Huge problems become manageable when you commit yourself to going forward. Just a little forward motion every day will add up, so keep that in mind when it feels like you're not making the progress you want.

Break It Down Into Simple Steps

One way to keep going forward is to break your problem down into simple steps. Every large undertaking is made up of a series of steps, make these as simple as possible, so that you can take one or two at a time and not feel overwhelmed. One tiny step at a time is still forward motion.

Don't Panic

The most important step of all. Depending on how large/unwieldy/seemingly impossible of a problem you have, you may be tempted to panic. Remembering the first two steps is one way to keep panic at bay. But also keep in mind that if it's your problem, you have the ability to handle it. Panicking will only make the problem seem impossible to solve. It's not.

The Small Tasks Of Life

I can't understand how the kitchen always needs to be cleaned—dirty dishes, crumbs on the floor, spills on the counters. I know most people eat at least three times a day, but still, I feel like I am constantly cleaning the kitchen.

Even though I love having a clean kitchen, I can't always bring myself to clean it up immediately after I've used it. It feels too tedious, too boring, too mundane. But eventually it needs to be done.

So I start cleaning it up, putting things back into the pantry, putting dirty dishes into the dishwasher, hand washing various pots and pans. Soon it's all done and it feels great, but what about the fifteen or so minutes that I spent with my hands in dishwater? Is it just a necessary evil?

Meditation

Despite (or maybe because of) the fact that they are routine, household chores can be meditative. It's not all about mantras and following your breath. Taking a routine activity and being present during it can be a form of meditation.

You don't have to use your brain much because chores are just manual labor. This is good for taking yourself out of your mind and away from your thoughts.

And, these tasks are the things that support life itself. Everyone has to eat, which means we all have to use the kitchen, which means cleaning it up and maintaining it are a part of nourishing our bodies, which means that doing the dishes is directly in support of life itself.

Exciting, Grand Moments

Hopefully you've had a few of these. Maybe you won a state championship when you were in high school. Maybe you landed your dream job, or traveled to a place that you always wanted to visit. We need some exciting moments when life seems to be more than we could have imagined.

But life doesn't consist of those moments. Really, they are few and far between (otherwise they wouldn't be exciting!). Which means that mostly our lives consist of small, routine, daily tasks. These are the bulk of our experience. And they are essential to our lives.

The Tasks That Support Life

I'm writing a novel. Actually it's already written. I'm now in the process of getting it ready to be published. There is a lot I don't know, a lot I've had to learn, and a lot of time and energy put towards this project.

I will be excited when this is all finished, when my book is completely ready for publication (I've been working on this for two years). But really, most of this process was mundane.

There were a few cool moments – like finishing the first draft and seeing the finished cover for the first time. But mostly, it was just me sitting down every day to write, writing 500 – 750 words, and then moving on with my day. Writing this book became just a part of my daily routine.

You need to have some exciting moments, and you will have them. But, remember, that's not what the bulk of your life consists of. Your life is not all champagne and reaching the summit of Mt. Everest, mostly, it's just doing the dishes.

When You Don't Know What You're Doing

I often find myself dreading situations where I feel like I don't know what I'm doing. I know it will be uncomfortable, and I may have to feel dumb for a while. And yet, in the end, I find that it has not only been rewarding, but enjoyable too.

Possibility

When you don't know what you're doing there is nothing to lean back on. This creates discomfort, but it also allows you to be much more open to possibilities. Things you probably would have missed otherwise.

When you've been doing something for a long time, you have a routine. You know where everything is going to be each step of the way, and that feels good because you don't have to expend a lot of energy.

But with too much comfort, seeing possibilities gets harder. When you don't know what you're doing, you have to take everything as it comes, and see what you can do with it. By remaining open, you spot possibilities easily.

Play

I find that when I lose the sense of play in my work (paid or otherwise) my stress levels begin to rise. When I play, I'm more open to learning, I'm more creative, and willing to take appropriate risks. When I don't play, I become rigid, focused on completing the task as fast as I can, and the task becomes joyless.

Not knowing what you are doing is a wonderful place to play. You are discovering boundaries, you are developing a system, and there is plenty of room to explore.

Fear cannot exist in Play. Becoming too attached to certain results makes us fearful. When we play, the results simply happen, whether we expected them or not. By being playful with your task, you push that fear out of the way, and allow yourself the opportunity to find the unexpected.

Enjoyment

When you don't know what you are doing, enjoyment is easy to come by. By being open to possibility and keeping a sense of play as you explore your activity, you engage with your activity at a deep level. This kind of depth creates a richness to all your moments. The kind of depth that tends to pass us by if we are not careful.

When you don't know what you are doing, each moment catches your attention because it has to. You've got to take each moment as it comes, feel it, explore it and live it, and not just get through it.

Each time I feel like I don't know what I'm doing, I find a freedom in "not knowing" that I wouldn't find in a familiar task. And, ultimately, I like that freedom, even if I have to feel dumb for a while to have it.

Get Rid of What You Don't Need

Just as there is a time to create more of what you want in your life, there is also a time to destroy what you don't want. When you think about improving your life you often focus on the things you would like to have but don't. You then focus on bringing those things into your life.

But you don't often think about the things you already have in your life that you need to get rid of. Many times you carry a lot of stuff with you that has outlived it's useful life. When that happens you need to destroy parts of your life before you can create more.

Be Like A Forest Fire

I'm sure there are many things you would like to create in your life, but what would you like to destroy? Are there skills you use regularly that you don't enjoy much? Are there people in your life who you just don't connect with anymore? Is your home filled with a bunch of stuff that you no longer use?

When you destroy parts of your life you are making room for new parts. You are making room for creation. Just like when a forest fire burns up the dead parts and makes room for new growth, you are destroying what is already dead so that new growth can occur.

Getting Rid Of Physical Stuff

My current "destruction" project is to de-clutter my apartment. I'm surprised that even in a relatively small space, so much stuff can sit around and not be used (or even remembered!).

Already, I've recycled/donated/thrown away magazines from 1995, papers from college, clothes I forgot I even had, out of date electronics, and books I had read once and hadn't looked at in 10 years. It's amazing the physical stuff that can pile up in your life.

Getting Rid Of Non-Physical Stuff

Most of us are carrying around with us an amazing amount of useless physical stuff, but what about less tangible things?

For instance, the way that we see ourselves is subject to creation and destruction. Hopefully the image that we carry of ourselves matches who we really are. But what if it doesn't?

A couple of years ago I quit a job that I hated. But along with the job, I was also quitting a vision that I had of myself, one that involved being what I thought "everyone" wanted me to be but that really didn't match my best self very well.

When I destroyed that vision of myself I opened my life up for new opportunities that much better suited me. I was carrying around a vision of who I was, that frankly, was not who I was. I burned it up in the fire, and something new grew in it's place.

Identify What You Don't Need

So how do you know which things you need to get rid of? Here are a few ways to tell that something needs to go from your life.

You've forgotten it even existed – This is mostly for the physical stuff that we have, but when you don't even remember that you own something, it's time to get rid of it. Someone else can probably make better use of it.

You're bored with it – This can be in regards to both physical and non-physical stuff. If you have something in your life that you once enjoyed but now find boring, it's time for that thing to go. Maybe you have run 3 miles everyday for the last

10 years. You enjoyed it at first and liked the challenge, but lately you just do it out of habit and are getting pretty bored with it. Maybe it's time to take up biking or swimming. Even though you want to continue your workouts, it's time for a new activity.

It feels like a chore – When parts of your life stop being enjoyable and start feeling like an item on your to-do list, it's probably time for that thing to go. Maybe you have a friend who you just don't feel as connected to anymore and hanging out with them is starting to feel like an obligation. Cutting down the amount of time you spend with them is probably a good idea because it makes room for a new, more fulfilling relationship.

It holds you back – Just like my example above of getting rid of a certain vision of myself, sometimes we hold onto a way of thinking that doesn't do us any good. What beliefs do you hold about yourself that limit your fulfillment? Do you have patterns in your life that seem to sabotage what you want? Take a look at the things that hold you back and then get rid of them!

PART TWO:

GOAL SETTING AND COMPLETING THINGS

The INFP's Guide To Goal Setting

Most of us have been exposed to the idea and practice of goal setting. And it goes something like this: (1) create a goal that is specific, measurable, and has a time limit; (2) create a plan to reach your goal, use objectives and action steps to fill in your plan; (3) follow your plan and measure your progress as you move towards your goal; (4) when you reach your goal, start over with a new one.

I have never been very good at this.

This is probably because of my personality preferences as an INFP. Specifically the P, which stands for Perceiving.

I find traditional goal setting practices to be constraining, and ultimately, I feel that it takes me away from my goals because of the level of specificity that is needed. My goals tend to be bigger, more open and not connected with a hard time limit. They are adaptable to whatever may come up and I will change them (or scrap them) as necessary. These things make me feel comfortable.

Essentially, when I create a goal, I will ask myself what I want to do for the upcoming year, 5 years, my life, etc. and write down exactly what that is, however it comes out of my brain. There is no censoring in this step. I don't worry if it's specific or measurable, I go with what I feel.

For instance, around the first of the year I was thinking about things I wanted to do in the upcoming year. One thing I came up with was to "receive love from others in a better way." That's pretty vague. I was thinking that I wanted to improve my relationships and I wanted to improve it in the way that I was receiving people. If I had tried to go more specific or make it measurable I would have actually walked away from what I really wanted. It was a feeling that was directing me, not specific actions or steps

I might revise a goal, but I revise it in a way that I feel something when I read it or say it. The most important thing to me is the feeling a goal gives me. That's how I know I'm on the right path.

You might ask how I know that I'm following my goal.

The first step is not to have too many of them. You need to be able to concentrate on a few. Next, if I'm holding the goal in my mind, when I come across a situation where the goal applies I can act in a way that satisfies the goal. If I want to receive people better, the next time I'm with a friend I have "receiving" in mind and can act in a number of ways that would satisfy that goal. With the goal open, there are an endless number of ways that the goal can be achieved. I like that.

You may also ask how I know that I've reached my goal.

If I'm holding it my mind and taking action on it when the situation arises, the goal takes care of itself. It is over when I feel that I'm doing a better job of receiving people. When I don't need to specifically think to myself "receive," then it's reached.

I feel very comfortable with this method of goal setting because it allows for so much possibility. The course of action is completely open, but I know what I'm walking towards. If I had to sum up my philosophy on goals it would be this:

A goal keeps you walking in the right direction, it doesn't dictate every step on your path.

If you find yourself feeling uncomfortable with traditional goal setting, maybe you need to try a new approach. Be looser, be vague, use your feelings and allow for possibility.

An Alternative To Goals

It's that time of year again when a lot of us create new goals and plans for how to reach them. The beginning of a new year is a hugely optimistic time and I think all of us do a lot of thinking about what we'd like to have or develop in the upcoming year.

Although I do spend time at the end of one year/beginning of the next thinking about things I'd like to have, do, or improve in the upcoming year, I have found myself settling into a much more fluid way of creating and achieving goals. So much so, that the term "goal" might not even be appropriate. (But, we don't need to be that nit-picky.)

Creating Goals

Part of my issue with goals is the setting of them in the first place. In the past, I might sit down at a specific time for the specific purpose of creating goals, maybe categorized by different areas of my life. But what I found was that my best goals sort of just "arose" in their own time.

When I sat down with the specific purpose of creating goals, sometimes they just felt uninspired or forced. So, even though it was the new year I might not come up with any goals that really made me feel something. My best goal that I created that year, may have popped into my mind while I was at the grocery store or sitting at my desk at work.

Goals and Desires and Swimming

Which brings me to my next point. The word "goal" has a very purposeful connotation, but, really, isn't a goal just a want or a desire? It just sounds a little better than saying, "here are my desires for the year." The word "desires" is a little fuzzier. But, for me, that's why I think I like it.

In the course of your days and weeks, you are exposed to so many things that it's almost impossible to not to have desires creep up on you. And these, I think, make the best goals.

A couple of years ago now, I'm not sure why, but the desire to do some swimming for exercise popped into my mind. Although I can swim, I'm not a swimmer—not for exercise or competition or anything more than wading in the ocean or enjoying a pool in the summertime. But the thought wouldn't leave me.

Over the next eight or nine months, the idea of swimming stayed with me, but I didn't have access to a pool and wasn't really sure how well I would do swimming laps—if I had the skill or endurance.

The thought kind of incubated in mind over these months, but I didn't take any action. It just didn't feel right. And then, one day, it felt right.

It was like, the idea had gestated and now felt ready to be put into action. I can't explain this really well. It's just a feeling that I get. I feel particularly energized and attracted to whatever it is that I want to do. Almost like I'm being pulled toward it and I can't stop that pull (but I don't want to).

I joined the local YMCA, bought an appropriate bathing suit and some goggles and got in the water. (By the way, I was pretty bad at first! I found lap swimming very difficult and had trouble making it one length of the pool. But there was something telling me to just keep going, so I did.)

Long story short, I started swimming, was not very good, but eventually was talking to another swimmer at the pool who recommended a "learn to swim" program that I did end up buying and following, and I'm happy to report that I've gotten a lot better and swimming is now much more enjoyable.

So, I guess you could say that I reached my goal in this situation. But the truth is that I'm not sure it was ever really a goal in the first place. Swimming was just a desire that arose one day for me, and I followed the feeling of that desire to it's completion. (And, really, there is no completion because I'm still swimming and still improving, and will always.)

Goals, Your Gut and The Road Ahead

Sometimes I think that setting goals requires you to "use your eyes" too much, rather than your gut. You look out into your life and see the things that are missing, and then you try to fill those in.

My goal of swimming didn't fill any particular purpose in my life. If I had sat down and taken a good look at my life, I wouldn't have seen learning to swim as filling in any holes in my life. It just came to me one day, and I couldn't let it go. The opportunity arose and I took it, even though it sort of came out of left field.

Goals can make you think that you've got everything under control. That you've planned it all out, and with perfect execution you can get exactly to where you thought you would go.

But then something happens. Maybe a good thing, maybe a bad thing, but a thing nonetheless and reaching your goal becomes that much more difficult. Or, you just don't have the motivation to follow it anymore. And you realize that no matter what you planned out, life sometimes just has different plans for you.

So, really, goals aren't necessary. You'll still have wants and desires (and if you want to call them goals, go ahead, this is really just a semantics thing and the way that I like to think about it), and if the opportunity arises and it feels right you can follow them. And if it stops feeling right, you can drop them. Or just maintain them without growing them. Anyway is fine.

I'm not really sure that at this point in my life I have goals anymore. I have things that I want, I have desires and I do follow them. But mostly, I see what comes up in front of me and take the opportunities that I get.

It feels good not to think that I can plan everything out and get there just the way I thought (although sometimes this thinking does creep back into my mind). And it's probably more realistic.

I'll get to where I'm going. It'll probably just be a really winding, twisty kind of road.

Setting Unreachable Goals

This is my first post of the new year and it's almost mandatory that I write about goals.

And I will write about goals, but I'll do it my way.

To start I want to say that this year I have a goal of posting a new blog post every week. And announcement posts don't count. I'm talking about a blog post on a particular topic that I want to write about, not that one of my books is on sale.

If you take a look at my archives, you will see that posting on this blog for the last five years or so has been intermittent at best. Once I got started writing fiction, and definitely once I started indie publishing, this blog went onto the back burner and I simply didn't write for it as much.

As a side note, this blog turns 10 this year! I started it in June 2008 with a somewhat-vague idea of it being a personal development/inspiration type blog and it was really fun and interesting for a while, especially considering that blogging was really popular then and I met a lot of other bloggers doing the same types of things that I was. But then I started writing fiction in the fall of 2009 and that quickly became my main focus. I knew I wanted to keep the blog, I just simply wasn't as active on it.

But anyway, back to the goal of posting once a week: Here's the thing, I know right now that I probably won't hit it. I'll be close, but will I put up 52 new blog posts this year? Unlikely.

And that's really the whole point. To pick something that is out of my reach and try to get as close to it as I can. In setting a goal you know you won't reach, you often end up further along than having set a more manageable, measurable goal.

Having a goal that's measurable is a goal-setting best practice, but I have always found this limiting because there is so much that can't be measured really. Setting a purposefully unreachable goal leaves room for more possibility, more things to surprise you.

I also have a tendency to slack off when it comes to meeting milestones. So, for instance, maybe posting 40 blog posts is actually a more manageable goal, but I'll see that 40 and hit 35 (I'm not sure why, it's just a personality thing I think), but if I see 52 then I might hit 47. So the goal that I know I'm not going to meet will take me further.

I have a friend who has a goal of being 100% serene all the time. Anyone who has lived on this planet for any length of time knows that this is completely unrealistic, but again that's the point. If that's the thing she's aiming for, she can continue to get closer and closer to it all the time without ever being able to reach it, but it keeps her progressing.

I guess it's like that quote about shooting for the moon and falling amongst the stars, unreachable goals have their value, even if you can't really measure them. And depending on your own personality you may actually find them more motivating.

Another great example is NaNoWriMo. Having a goal of 50,000 words in a month is a lot and out of the four times I've participated, I've only hit the goal once. But in the other years, I may have hit 25,000 or 35,000 and that's still a lot for a month (for me), so having that big goal keeps me moving along and ends up being very productive even when I don't meet it.

So in a year I'll see where I am with the blog posts. But I can tell you this, I'm going to be blogging a lot more this year and you never know, I may just hit that 52, and next year I'll have to double the number.

Getting It Done

I have a tendency to want to make things perfect, or at least very high quality.

But the thing about perfect or very high quality is that it takes a lot of time and energy. Maybe more than I actually have. So I've learned to focus on getting things done with a level of quality that is at least adequate, but usually more than adequate, even though it's not perfect.

This is not my natural way of wanting to do things, but its been an adjustment that I've needed to make if I want to advance in certain areas of my life. Not to mention that it's a lot less stressful than trying to make things perfect.

For example, I was working a graphic the other day that displays at the bottom of posts to draw attention to the fact that I have free short stories available to be downloaded.

After a little while of playing around with it, I began to question it in a number of ways. The gradient in the text felt like it could use some tweaking. I wasn't sure if I needed a button or other text to get more clicks on it. Was it explanatory enough? Or did I need some more text?

But as I questioned it more and more, I recognized something. It had reached a level of adequacy, my gut feeling told me to leave it alone for now, and I could always make changes/improve upon it later.

It was totally fine to go up on my website, and to continue to tinker with it would probably just make me a little insane. Because with anymore tinkering I would be trying to get it "perfect" on the first try rather than getting something done that needed to get done—namely a graphic that was pointing people in the direction of my free short stories.

As a one-woman indie author show, there are things that just have to get done where I can't spend the time and energy that I naturally want to. It's okay. It will be fine. (I tell myself.) It's more important to get these things done than it is to try and make them perfect.

Because also, perfect doesn't really exist. I like to think it does. And I like to think I can get there on the very first try(!) but really it's just an abstract concept where I think all my problems will be solved and nothing bad will happen.

Letting go of perfect can be difficult. But, really, when I'm striving for perfect I'm denying myself all of the really cool things that can happen if I just get it done.

"Good Enough" Is Underrated

As a recovering perfectionist, I've had to change my relationship with "good enough."

I used to believe that "good enough" didn't exist. There was perfect or close-to-perfect and that was all that mattered. "Good enough" seemed downright mediocre and self-loathing. Why would anyone do something at a "good enough" level?

But at my last job, I started to learn something. Trying to do all my work at near-perfect levels wasn't getting me anywhere. It was getting me plenty of stress, and in a weird way it was actually decreasing my work performance.

See, the thing was, I was putting too much energy into work assignments, completing them in a way that I thought was high quality but in actuality wasn't adding much value to the completed work.

I began to see it this way: I always wanted to operate at a 9 or a 10. But in most instances, a 6 or a 7 was perfectly fine. Going those extra few points was really just draining my energy and making it less likely that things were getting done in a timely fashion.

Working on something until it was "good enough" and then getting it out the door saved me a lot of stress and kept my work moving along. "Good enough" was a much better option than close-to-perfect.

In my writing and publishing it's the same thing. Writing a "good enough" blog post every week is better than writing a close-to-perfect one every once in a while. Writing a "good enough" story for my newsletter every month is way better than not sending one at all because the story isn't perfect. Publishing a book at a "good enough" level is much better than not publishing at all, because there will be readers who will be happy I shared rather than holding back, and because in self-publishing I can change just about anything at anytime, so I can always improve on it.

Ultimately, doing things at a "good enough" level allows me to show up on a regular basis, and I believe that showing up is more important than doing everything perfectly.

The Importance of Completing Things

I'm a great starter. I love to start things. It's exciting, new and my energy is high.

I'm also a pretty decent finisher. Mostly because when you finish something then you get to start something new.

But it's in the middle where I start to have issues.

In the middle, the novelty and excitement of a new thing has worn off, and the end is still a ways off. I find that where I sprint off at the beginning, in the middle I'm starting to drag my feet, trying to find the energy to keep moving forward.

Honestly, I just find middles a little boring. Which is why when I start something, I always make completion my goal. Otherwise I will start several things and never finish them. And then they will be sitting around, and I will never do anything with them.

When I commit to completing things, I grow during that activity because I have to take that thing from beginning to end, and endure all the parts in between. Also, at the end, I have something to show for myself, even if it's not very good. That's a risk you take when you start something, though.

But the good news is, once you complete something and you start in on something new of the same sort, you now know the drill, and the second (or third, or fourth, or fifth) time around you have a better idea of what you are doing. And you improve.

But completion is instrumental in the improvement. I don't think you are going to get the growth you want, without the completion.

If you know what NaNoWriMo is, you know that the goal is to write a novel in a month, which sounds crazy—and it is. But the whole point is to complete it, not to make it good quality, which seems like a really odd objective, but if you think about it, it's not.

Many people never start the things that they want to do because they are afraid that it won't be any good. So NaNoW-riMo allows writers to go through the exercise of completing that novel that they've been thinking about, and lets them worry about quality later.

Because, probably, the kind of quality you are looking for won't come for you on the first go-round. It will only come after completing a few things first.

And once you have a few completions under your belt, you won't even notice the improvement that snuck up on you.

When Your Goals Seem Far Away

All of us have goals. Many of us have (mostly) clear goals that we've written down, with a plan that we think will get us there. But, we often distrust our own decision making, particularly when we come to a fork in the road and it's not clear which way will lead us towards what we want. Will I chose the correct fork? Or will I make a terrible decision that will lead me far away from where I want to be?

Decision making doesn't need to be this stressful. Putting aside your self doubt, you can learn to trust what you already have, and know that you already have everything you need.

When I have a goal that seems daunting and I'm not sure how to get there, I take it one step at a time, and I keep two things in mind:

- **You can only act on things that you have already thought of. If you can't think to do it, then you can't take action.**

- **You can only act with the resources you already have.**

When I ask myself what is the next step I need to take to reach this goal, I don't worry about steps I can't think of. I don't worry about what I might be missing, because what I miss is of no use to me. I trust what I already have and I know that my next action must come from my thoughts.

Even if the thought is "I will ask advice from So-and-So" and they give me some helpful ideas on what action to take, the action (asking advice) came from my thoughts. Don't worry about all the things you can't think of—take action on what you can.

Likewise, I can't act with resources that I don't have. So, my thoughts, the relationships I have with other people, my skills and abilities, actual physical resources I might have (equipment, space, etc.)—these are all things that I can use to take action towards my goals. But, if I don't have it now, then I can't use it to take my next step.

What this means is no matter how big your goal is, your next step has to come from things you have around you right now. The next step of your goal is always in reach, which means that ultimately your goal is in reach. (Although, how much time it will take you don't know.) The further you go towards your goal, the broader your knowledge and resources will be (assuming you are learning along the way!), and you will be able to take more skilled actions as you go along.

Don't worry about the things you don't have, focus on what you do have and figure out a way to use those things in the best possible way. You already have what you need.

The Heavy Ball

I played basketball in high school.

Sometimes at practice my coach would pull out the heavy balls, which were, you guessed it, heavier than a regular basketball. I'm not sure exactly how much they weighed, but they were significantly heavier than the regular basketball.

And we would do our normal drills.

Only with the heavy ball, things that were normally easy for us became hard.

Even passing to a teammate a short distance away might be a struggle, and shooting the ball? Forget it.

But when we put the heavy balls away and went back to the regular balls it was like we had super strength. Everything became easier.

Because that's the thing about doing it the hard way for a while. Afterward, things that were hard are now easy.

So maybe from time to time you might want to think about pulling out your heavy ball.

But only if you want super strength, that is.

PART THREE:

DECISION MAKING

Does It Resonate?

There's a lot of advice out there. Whether you are a writer, a painter, an entrepreneur, a parent or a DIY home improvement person, you'll find advice—and usually far too much of it.

I mean, on the one hand it's great. If you're looking for information or support, you'll definitely find it, but you also have to sift through it, and, frankly, some of it will simply not apply to you or will be bad advice (for you, at least) for a number of reasons.

So what's a human being to do who wants to figure something out but doesn't want the mental overload?

See If It Resonates

Do you know what that feeling is? When something resonates with me I feel it in my body, my mind and my intuition.

In my body, there is a release of tension and an ease in my breathing. In my mind, I may get excited, curious, or interested. And my intuition gives me that "pull." That's when I know something is resonating, and is right for me to act on.

Whatever You Do, Don't Do Your Own Book Cover Design... Or Else

This tends to be the typical advice that indie authors hear when researching book cover design—get a professional to do it, don't do it yourself or you will have disastrous results. But it never resonated with me.

I was very interested in doing my own book cover designs. Something about it just called out to me. And most importantly, I was willing to learn and to practice. And that's exactly what I did.

My first several designs weren't awesome, but I started to get the hang of it after a while and then I kept on improving. I feel fairly confident in my ability to design a book cover these days (and other graphics too) but I found it really difficult to go against the dominant advice surrounding book covers. If I hadn't resonated so strongly with it, I would have never been able to do it.

Obviously, this is an example of resonating against certain pieces of advice. But what about resonating with?

Look For The Thing That Jumps Out At You

Like everyone else on the planet these days, I read a lot of articles/blog posts, listen to podcasts, watch a bunch of videos, etc. And I'm always looking for the information that I want to keep, so to speak.

If I'm reading a blog post, for instance, I don't follow it to the letter–no matter how knowledgeable or experienced that person is, I'm looking for the piece that jumps out at me. You know that sentence or paragraph that seems to leap off the page? I'll probably feel some excitement about it and my body relaxes. I know that this is something I should file away.

The rest of the post may not work for me at all, and that's fine. If I take away one good thing from a blog post, that's a success! (For me and for the blogger.) This way, I'm not drowning in information, trying to figure out what applies to me. I'm being selective and letting my intuition guide the way.

Will It Hurt Anything?

I can be indecisive. I think that's pretty typical for INFPs (and human beings in general, as well).

I like to take my time with decisions. Let my intuition weigh in. Give my subconscious a good chance to process through it. Maybe even do something crazy like a little research or weighing out the pros and cons.

And for many things, this works just fine. But sometimes I'm not getting a real clear direction to go in, and this is when the over-analyzing starts.

Should I do this? Should I do that? There's this thing I want to do, but I don't know if I should go for it.

And this can go on for quite a while if I let it. But what I've realized is that sometimes I need to just make a decision even if I don't feel completely clear on the direction. Otherwise it's too easy to get stuck.

And one thing I do to get myself moving is to ask myself:

Will it hurt anything to do this?

If the answer is no, then I can plow ahead with my best decision and just see what happens, because, you know, it's not going to hurt anything.

Now if the answer is maybe or yes, then you've got a different situation on your hands, and that's not the subject of this blog post.

But if the answer is a no, then what have you got to lose? Go ahead, make that decision, and see what happens.

At least you're not still stuck over-analyzing.

How To Figure Out What To Do Next

The amount of choice we have is overwhelming.

When it's time to make a decision about which step to take next, we are often paralyzed with indecision. Not wanting to make the wrong choice, but not knowing which one is right, we stand at the fork in the road and don't choose either direction.

There is an incredibly simple way to pick a direction and start walking.

Pick the easiest next step you can think of.

That's right. The easiest. Not the hardest or the most sophisticated-seeming, but the easiest choice you can make that will take you forward.

Often when we start something and the result we want is the product of a long and complicated process, we kind of freak out. Because at that moment it's too overwhelming to think about all the things we will need to do to get there. Probably, we don't even know all the things we need to do to get there.

At this point we might just stop, not ever getting started, because it just seems like too much. But we are missing something obvious when we do this.

If you always take the easiest next step, the one that seems too obvious to mean anything, eventually those steps add up, and you develop sophistication along the way, and you are able to take more and more complicated steps because you've been building upon what you know along the way.

Those easy steps add up, and you have something bigger than you ever thought you would have.

And remember, easy is relative. What was easy to you at the beginning is much less sophisticated than what you consider easy now.

Take the path of ease.

How To Use Your Gut Feeling

There are two ways to make decisions. One is with your eyes. The other is with your gut.

Gut feelings are stronger, quicker, and lead to better results than anything your eyes could ever tell you.

A Sensation In Your Body

A gut feeling is appropriately named because the sensation feels like it is actually coming from your gut. It isn't a bodily sensation in the way that hunger or pain are bodily sensations. Gut feelings are not physical in origin. But the sensation you do feel seems to originate in your gut.

Also, a gut feeling might actually come from another place in your body (your heart, for instance), but the point is that this is a feeling that arises from your body, but is not of your body.

It Doesn't Always Match Your Eyes

What your eyes see and what your gut sees are often two very different things. Your gut might tell you to go for something that your eyes are telling you is dangerous, risky or will cause you embarrassment. Your eyes tend to get caught up in things like that. But your gut sees right past those things to the fulfillment that lies beyond.

Your gut doesn't necessarily lead you towards the easiest path, but it always leads you towards the one that will give you increased life—the feeling of being more alive. Don't let your eyes lead you astray.

Relief vs. Tension

You know you have satisfied your gut when you feel relief after making a decision. You will get this sensation even if you are afraid of what your gut is telling you to do. The relief comes from knowing you are on the right path.

On the other hand, if you choose against your gut feeling, you will feel tension in that area. Even if you feel temporarily safer by going against your gut, that tension tells you that you are going in the wrong direction.

What To Do When You Feel Stuck

When you feel stuck, the first thing you want to do is struggle. Flailing about, throwing your weight around, trying harder and harder, pushing against the resistance you feel. Only these things don't get you unstuck. In fact, they tend to make you sink deeper into whatever problem you are trying to solve.

From time to time we all have problems that seem to take on a life of their own. We try to solve them, but the solution doesn't come easy. We try harder to solve the problem, but the harder we try, the more we feel like we are getting no where. This is feeling stuck.

Quicksand

Think of it like quicksand. (I've never actually been in quicksand, but I do watch survival shows.) If you step into quicksand you start to sink. When you start to sink, you begin to panic. When you begin to panic, you start to struggle against the quicksand, trying to pull yourself out of it, but by doing that, you only sink deeper.

It's only when you stop, and try to increase the amount of body surface that is touching the quicksand (by laying as much of yourself flat as you can) that you can get out of the quicksand. But, this method is not at all your first instinct. It requires slowing down, assessing the situation and then using your brain, not your muscles, to get you out.

Getting Un-Stuck

When you feel stuck, follow these steps for optimal problem solving:

Stop – A really simple first step. When you notice that you are "sinking," stop struggling immediately. You don't want to sink any further.

Define the problem – This may seem unnecessary or a waste of time, but knowing exactly what the problem is helps us take the correct action. Also, sometimes there is a problem behind the problem. You need to know which one to work on first, but also which one is the "root" problem.

Focus on the present – Don't worry about things that have already happened, for instance, what you "should have done" to avoid the problem. It may be true, but at this point, it's not helpful to dwell on it. Once you are unstuck, you can go back and reflect on patterns and behavior that lead to the problem, but in the heat of the moment, it's not something to focus on. If you are stuck in quicksand don't worry about the wrong turn you took that lead you there, focus on getting out.

Focus on solutions – Focusing on solutions will lead you toward a solution. Focusing on the problem will lead you back to the problem. Solutions energize you.

What can I do next? – Every huge problem or task is simply a series of small steps. Figure out which small step you need to take next. Size honestly doesn't matter here. Even the smallest step forward will count. Keep asking yourself "What can I do next?" until you are done. Moving forward steadily (not necessarily quickly) will eventually get you to your solution.

Getting Myself Un-Stuck

When I had finished school several years ago and was looking for a job, after a few months I really began to feel stuck. I wasn't finding any jobs that really appealed to me, and the jobs I interviewed for felt all wrong. I felt that I was looking in all the wrong places and the more I looked and applied, the farther away I felt from where I wanted to be.

When I finally took a moment to stop and assess where I was, I could see that I really had two problems that were getting in each other's way. One was that I simply needed to be employed and earn money, so I could get an apartment and pay my bills. That was the immediate problem. But the other problem was that I was struggling with what I really wanted to do with my life. What kind of career did I want to go into? What was I passionate about? What kind of life did I want to live? This was the "root problem," and it was getting in the way of my immediate one.

After I had teased those two problems out from one another, I could focus on present solutions to my immediate problem. When I thought about what I needed most, I realized that I needed some sort of temporary job while I was still looking for something more permanent. After I had done that I focused myself on looking for a job that would allow me to practice or develop some skill that I wanted, but that wasn't perfect.

With my temporary job in place, I didn't feel so pressured to find a job, and could be a bit more methodical in my search. Also, I put my question of what made me really passionate off to the side, and worked on that separately from my immediate job search.

I was making this problem bigger than it was by struggling too much. When I stepped back and looked at the problem as a series of steps, it seemed manageable, all of the sudden. And, in the end, it turned out fine.

When you feel stuck, your problems tend to feel huge and unmanageable. Taking some time to assess the situation and look at what small steps you need to take helps you feel capable of taking on the challenge.

Now, the next time you step in quicksand, you will know what to do.

Use Self Reflection To Get Some Direction

Have you ever done something and then thought to yourself, "Why did I do that"? Have you ever wondered to yourself how you will ever get to where you want to be, or even where it is that you want to be?

Taking the time to properly reflect on your life is a practice that will help you understand yourself. Here are some things you need in order to do that.

Find the Right Environment

First and foremost, every good reflector knows that the environment in which you reflect is extremely important. Since you are spending time with yourself it needs to be private. Generally, it also needs to be quiet and physically comfortable for you.

You need a space where you can always come back to your self. This space doesn't necessarily need to be physical, although it could be that your space is a room in your house or in another building, or a place out in nature, or a basketball court where you go to shoot hoops (alone), but it could also be a certain time of day or having certain objects around you that evoke certain feelings.

Wherever or whatever this space is, it just needs to be a place where you can have a productive meeting with yourself.

Ask Yourself Questions

Now that you have the right environment, you can start with the substance of reflection. Question yourself. If you want to keep this very simple there are only two questions you need to ask: What is going well for me? What is not going well for me? Another way of asking these questions is to ask: What have I done that energizes me? What have I done that takes energy away from me?

When you reflect, do so on a certain time period. If you are reflecting everyday, examine the past day of your life. If you are doing this every week, then you would use the past week. Apply your questions to the time period.

You could also use this time to create goals or check in on your progress on already existing goals. You could create a set a questions that you ask yourself every time you reflect that are more detailed than the two above.

If you are a less structured kind of person you could simply use this time to "free associate." Ask yourself the above two questions and see where your thoughts lead you. Or you could spend time visualizing the attainment of your goals or how you would like your life to look.

Most of all, notice how you feel as you look back on certain aspects of your life or when you are checking in with your goals or when you are visualizing your ideal life. Your feelings can tell you a lot about what you need to change and what you need to stick with.

Record Your Thoughts

What do you do with the information that you receive about yourself? Record it. Many people record their reflections in a journal, but writing is not the only way to record your reflections. You could make a video of yourself or record yourself, you could paint, draw, or sculpt. You could probably even dance or do something else physical. Put your reflection in a form that has meaning to you.

Recording what you learn is just a way of giving physical form to your thoughts and feelings. It doesn't necessarily have to be a record you can go back to, although it could be.

Effortless Decision Making

Anytime I have ever made a really important decision in my life and the results were favorable, it was generally because I went along with a strong feeling that I had that wasn't based on much concrete information. Generally, lists of pros and cons (and other similar methods) don't usually work for me when I have a choice to make because I prefer to use my intuition. From my observations, I find that a lot of people agonize over whether or not they are making the right decision and spend a lot of time poring over the facts to no avail. Intuitive decision making tends to be less painful and quicker, but requires a little risk taking.

I'm not saying other methods don't work, I'm only saying I don't prefer to use them. So, if making a pros and cons list works for you, stick with that. But, if you are interested in using a more intuitive approach here are some steps that I take.

Go With What You Are Drawn To

There's probably a good reason that you are attracted to it. Something about it has gotten you interested—trust yourself and go see what it is. In my experience, what we are drawn to is generally what is right for us at that time. Besides, would you ever go after something that repels you? Or, that you felt apathetic about?

Feel Your Way Along

Earlier this year, I tried out indoor rock climbing for the first time. I was in a class where the instructor had us climb blindfolded (not on the very first time!) and, oddly enough, I found it to be easier. When I was climbing and using my eyes, I would look at a hand/foot hold and think to myself "I can't put my foot there, it's not big enough." But when I had no eyes, I also had no judgments. I simply felt my way up the wall, putting my feet and hands where I could, based simply on touch.

If we give too much authority to our eyes, sometimes we miss things along the way.

Which One Can You Not Accept?

This is for really difficult choices. When you are faced with two choices and neither of them seem particularly appealing, decide which one you cannot accept and choose the other. Many times, in this situation, one of the choices really sucks and the other one you are simply afraid to do. Deciding what you can absolutely not accept in your life leads you to the right decision—even if it's something you are afraid to do.

Trust Yourself!

Making decisions based on intuition ultimately requires that you trust yourself and your feelings. It's the difference between using your eyes to do everything and using your body to feel your way along. Take the leap! Why would you lead yourself astray?

The Use of Self Discipline

Many of us wish we were more self-disciplined. If we could only will ourselves to do what we needed to do when we needed to do it, we would be successful, fulfilled and have the things that we always wanted. Think of the last lazy weekend afternoon when there were errands to run, chores to finish and maybe a personal project or two that you wanted to work on. Yet all you wanted to do was lay around and watch old movies on TV or spend time outside with your family. In those moments we wish that our willpower was ironclad and we could push the thought of movies or sunshine out of our minds.

But, what if, despite the errands and the chores and the projects, what you really needed to do that afternoon was lay around or spend time outside? How do you decide between what must get done and what you desire to do?

Following your own desire can be exhilarating, but also a bit scary. Imagine what it would be like if you said "yes" to everything that you wanted to do when you wanted to do it. Your life would be much more enjoyable, but most of us would be afraid that we were telling ourselves the "wrong things" to do. We have received a message that what we want will lead us down the wrong path, and the remedy for this is harsh self-discipline—the ability to force yourself to constantly do things you don't want to do.

When our bodies need fuel, we get a message in the form of hunger. When our bodies need to rest, we get a message in the form of sleepiness. If we listen properly, our body tells us exactly what it needs and I don't feel that this is any different from looking out of your window and desiring to go outside rather than work. We tell ourselves what we need when we need it, even for things that aren't "essential" for the maintenance of our bodies.

Maybe on that lazy afternoon, what you really need is fresh air and sunshine, physical activity, time with your family and play. And, when you think about it, the errands you want to do aren't a necessity, and the chores you can finish during the week and there really is no rush on your personal project. In this case, I feel following your intuition is the right thing to do. So shake off your guilty feeling and go outside.

On the other hand, maybe you desperately need to go to the grocery store or you will be eating out of drive-thru windows this upcoming week. I think this is the time when our brains kick in and tell our bodies to hold on a minute. Yes, the sun is shining, but you are really trying to eat healthier and a week of fast food just isn't going to cut it. Having some self discipline in this case is a good thing and ultimately will serve you as well as your body does when it needs something.

Your brain and your body aren't enemies—they just have different roles. And you can use both to pick the direction you need to walk in. I think I prefer the term "self-management" for this process, rather than "self-discipline." To me, "self-discipline" infers that you have to punish yourself to keep yourself in line. Or that you have to force yourself to do the "right things." But, "self-management" implies a back and forth process between your body and your mind. You can discern between when you need to follow your body and when you need to follow your mind. You are in charge of yourself, but you know when to listen also.

PART FOUR:

SCHEDULING AND PLANNING

"Scheduling" For INFPs

As an INFP, I like talking about how I get things done because it's different than the way a lot of other people do things. The point isn't that I'm special or anything, it's just that I've had to experiment to find out what works for me because the "typical" way doesn't often work.

I was talking with an INFP friend about writing/work schedules recently and we discussed the idea of using "intentions" rather than scheduling things at a certain day/time so that the to-do item could be on our minds rather than strictly scheduled.

The way that this works is to set a work intention for the week or the day and then you let yourself be pulled toward it at the right time.

This "pull" is important for INFPs and over the years I've tried to learn the best way to work with it.

Ultimately, I use structure to give me the most space possible so that I can then go in any direction I want to. Take the writing of this blog post for instance.

On my calendar, every Tuesday afternoon there is a block for "Write Blog Post" because I aim to post a blog post on Wednesday morning every week. Now, this is a little bit of a trick because blog posts don't always get written on Tuesday afternoons, nor do they always get posted on Wednesday mornings. But they will generally get posted by the end of the week. For instance, it is now Thursday afternoon.

But anyways—Tuesday afternoon came and went this week and I did not write a blog post even though I saw it there on the calendar because there was something else I wanted to do (and at this point I can't even remember what that was).

Wednesday afternoon however, I was ready to write a blog post so I sat down and started writing. I got about halfway through before I saw something on my website that needed attention, so I abandoned the blog post to take care of that. No problem. It's still only Wednesday afternoon and I just need to get something posted by Friday. And I was glad to take care of that thing on my website.

And now it's Thursday afternoon and I'm finishing up this post and will get it posted afterward, so I've made my weekly blog post in a circuitous but ultimately, finished, way.

The thing is that having it on the calendar reminds me that it needs to get done every week, but I know that it won't necessarily get done on a Tuesday/Wednesday but it will get written and posted by Friday.

If it's not on the calendar, it may not be on my mind enough to actually get it done, and I really like doing a blog post once a week. But if it's scheduled too tightly, I may miss out on something else pulling at me on that time and day. Simple, right?

My INFP-Style To-Do List

So this is another one of my INFP-style productivity posts. I had written one about goal setting several years ago and now I will examine the practice of making a to-do list and how I, in my INFP-ness, approach this.

The to-do list is a staple of any productivity plan. Generally, it is created and completed in an analytical manner, taking care to prioritize the tasks of the day and making sure that they get done.

Well, welcome to my to-do list…

At the start of each work day, I sit down and think to myself: what absolutely needs to get done today? And I see what comes to mind.

Now, here's something very important—I don't write any of this down. Nowhere in the making of my to-do list do I actually write anything down, and believe it or not, I find this much less stressful than it's opposite.

Okay, so back to what absolutely must get done today. I see what comes to mind and generally I come up with one or two things. This part is incredibly important. When thinking of the most essential tasks of the day, it can't be very many things, otherwise each task becomes less and less essential.

When I think of what must get done today, it could be something that's attached to a deadline or it could be something that must get done before I can move forward with something else. There may be some other criteria I use as well, but because I'm doing this intuitively I don't always know. I go by feeling. That tells me what is essential for the day.

So once I have that very short mental list, I know that these one or two things are the minimum of what I need to get done that day. If I do nothing else but those tasks I will be moving forward. And what that means is anything else I do is gravy.

The other thing I do here is figure out when during the day I'm going to do them. Just because a task is essential doesn't mean it's very big or takes a lot of energy. I reserve mornings for higher energy tasks, and afternoons for lower energy tasks, so I fit in my essential tasks where I need them.

Okay, cool. Now that I have that very simple plan, I start in on my day. For me, that means asking "what's next?" over and over until I'm done.

However, like I said earlier, I keep in mind that I need to go with the flow of my daily energy, which for me means, things that require more energy in the morning and things that require less energy in the afternoons.

So in the morning when I ask "what's next?" I limit myself to higher energy activities and in the afternoon when I ask that question, I'm picking from lower energy activities.

I know I'm done for the day when I ask "what's next?" and nothing comes to mind. And I'm a firm believer that if I've reached the point where nothing else needs to get done, I stop working and go live the rest of my life.

So there you have it—my to-do list where nothing gets written down and I move forward by intuition and feeling. Works for me.

What's Next?

I'm not much of a planner. Never have been.

I might make a list or two. Maybe even work with some kind of very loose plan or outline, but mostly I just like to follow along with my intuition.

Generally, I'll just ask myself "What's next?" as in "What's the next step?"

This goes for life as well as writing.

Because I prefer to follow my intuition and because I prefer to keep things open to possibilities, making concrete plans often makes me feel a little constrained. Using the "What's next?" strategy, I keep myself moving along, while staying open to possibilities—often things I never saw coming (which I love).

Even with a large project or task, simply asking yourself "What's next?" works just fine, because, if you think about it, you can only ever take the next step. I can't take the step four steps from now. I'll take that when I get there. I only have to worry about what's next, because steps, by their nature, build upon one another.

The beauty of this is that while you're only taking the next step, steps add up. Faster than you might think.

If you take one step every day, by the end of the week you've taken seven steps, and by the end of the month thirty. That can really add up.

So, if you're like me and you don't work that well with traditional planning methods, maybe you don't need to. Maybe you just need to ask yourself: "What's next?"

Sticking To The Plan vs. Going With The Flow

There are two opposing forces at work when I write, in terms of productivity.

One, I want to keep moving forward in a timely manner with my projects, and, two, I want to follow my creative/energetic rhythms.

If I'm too goal oriented, I may miss out on something great that I only would have found going with the flow. But, if I'm not goal oriented enough, projects may drag out unnecessarily, taking way too long to finish them.

By nature I'm more of a go-with-the-flow kind of person. I'd prefer to simply follow my intuition on how and what to work on. But I've found that doing a little planning and scheduling helps me move things forward. Gives me a little balance.

So I was thinking this morning—I had planned for the month of June to mostly be time to work on my novel, which means that I would work on it during my peak creative/energetic time which happens to be in the morning. So right now, for instance, according to my plan, I should be working on my novel. But I just didn't feel like it this morning.

When I get like this I try to discern if this means I should really work on something else outside the plan or do I just sit down, open up whatever it is I'm supposed to be working on, and get to it even though I don't totally feel like it.

In the case of this morning, I REALLY didn't feel like working on the novel. The energy was telling me it just wasn't there. And there were some other things I felt pulled to work on. However, sometimes the opposite happens.

Like, I'm generally feeling a little unenthusiastic and un-excited about my scheduled activity but I feel the best course of action is just to sit down and get started and after a little while I'll probably get into it. I just need to push myself a little to get started.

So there you have it. My little push/pull drama that plays out on a regular basis.

Leaving Space In Your Day

Do you ever feel like life is yanking you around by the neck?

It's pretty easy to feel like that. There are many demands on our time and people who need things from us. But feeling like you are on a treadmill that you can't turn off and is only going faster and faster isn't very pleasant.

One thing I've done over the years to combat this feeling is to leave some space between activities. To take a minute (like, actually sixty seconds) to sit quietly and breathe, maybe look out the window, and rest, without rushing off to the next activity.

One other benefit of doing this is that it helps with my work flow. Often times when I'm sitting there doing nothing, the next activity that I'd like to do pops into my mind and I get excited about working on it (or maybe not excited-excited, especially if it's like, "go fold the laundry" but there's at least the feeling of flow between activities). Whereas jumping from activity to activity can often make my work flow a little less deliberate because it's more reactionary.

So, here's what this looks like. Let's say I'm in the process of writing a story and there are plenty of other writing-related or publishing activities to do later. When I'm finished writing, instead of leaping right away into that next activity, I'll close all the open windows on my computer. I don't actually shut my laptop, but I close out all the browser tabs and open folders and whatever else I had open so I'm just looking at my background.

Next, I may stay seated, but turn away from my desk, put my feet up on the window sill and watch what's going on outside the window. There's a tree right there, so there are often birds around. There may be neighbors outside and I might watch them a moment (though I try not to go too Rear Window on anyone.) And maybe I focus in on my breathing, just noticing my inhales and exhales.

If I want to get really advanced, I may actually stand up, find my little basketball and shoot a few hoops at the toy hoop in my office. It gets me into my body and takes my mind off of whatever I was working on before or what I need to work on later.

At this point, a minute or two or three may have passed and I can get back to work, but I'm more refreshed than I would have been otherwise and ready to focus again.

Of course, the truth is, I don't always do this. Sometimes, I'm so caught up in what I'm doing that I do go rushing off into the next activity, and then the one after that too. But I have found that this kind of rushing tends to increase my stress, so I really do try to leave those spaces in my day. And, honestly, what are we rushing to anyway?

How To Have More Time

Time is the one thing that you never have enough of, right? Wrong. There is plenty of time.

Use time, don't let it use you.

Do The Thing You Feel "Pulled" To Do

Don't let your calendar or to-do list rule your life. By all means, have both of those things, but let them be guidelines for how you spend your time, rather than rigid rules.

Here's what you should do (note: requires a bit of courage)—take a look at your calendar and then make your to-do list. Then put both of those things aside (no peeking).

Sit quietly for a moment and ask yourself, "what needs to be done next?" Do whatever pops into your mind first, whatever you feel the strongest urge to do, even if it's not first on your list.

If you are worried that you will never do the things that must be done, I assure you that when you look in the kitchen and the dirty dishes are overflowing the sink, you will feel an urge to do the dishes. Or if you have a deadline approaching at work, you will feel an urge to do the next thing that will get you to completion. Don't worry, it will all get done.

Take A Break

One of the best ways to free yourself of the tyranny of time is to take a break.

There's so much to do that you couldn't possibly think of taking a break, right? Wrong. Take that break.

If you feel the urge to rest (see above), do it. This lets Time know that you cannot be ruled by it. You will use it as you see fit, and right now it's time to take a walk.

Focus On Now

Be here. Right now.

What are you doing this very moment? Whatever it is, just do that thing.

Use your senses. What do you hear right now? What are you tasting right now? (I think you get the point).

If you start to have thoughts of other things that are not present now, notice them, then gently let them go and once again, focus on now. (Meditation can help you practice this.)

It is always now. And when you think of it like that, time is nothing but now, which seems to pass with the circumstances, but maybe it really doesn't. Maybe it's always right now.

And, that, you have plenty of.

PART FIVE:

EMBRACING UNCERTAINTY

I Don't Know

Once upon a time (back in 2006) I had my first full-time job post-Masters Degree. I didn't get paid a lot but I did take away (at least) one gem that has paid me many times over since then. Here it is:

When you don't know something, say "I don't know."

Amazing, huh?

This very simple, but not necessarily easy to follow, piece of advice was essential to my job of being a trainer (as in, on-the-job training, not personal training) as I was in front of a classroom full of people on many days.

The temptation to give some kind of answer—any kind of answer—to people who asked a question you didn't know the answer to was high. But one of the more experienced trainers always used to tell us to just say "I don't know. I'll find out and get back to you" or something to that effect, because the alternative usually didn't lead to anything good.

If upon being asked a question you didn't know the answer to, you were compelled to give a bullshit answer just to make it look like you knew what you were talking about, people inevitably knew that they were being lied to. Always. Every time. And it would affect your classroom management.

Trying to make it seem like you knew everything would always backfire. It was much easier (if not a little humbling) to just say "I don't know." The funny thing was that people tended to respect that answer. Probably because you were simply being straightforward with them.

Not everything is knowable. Not everything is knowable right now. Many times "I don't know" is the most truthful answer we have even if it's not the one we want to hear.

In a classroom full of irritable trainees it might have gone over pretty well, but sometimes "I don't know" just doesn't seem to cut it in our personal lives, in our communities or in our respective cultures.

But oftentimes, it's the only true answer we have.

There Is No Place To Get To

We often think, at any given point in our lives, that we are going somewhere. That there is some place we have to get to.

Maybe we want to reach a milestone in our careers or personal relationships. Or maybe we reach a certain age and feel that certain things need to be accomplished by then. Maybe we have a dream that we would like to see realized, something we've wanted for a long time. Something we are sure will make our lives better.

And, maybe, you actually reach that milestone or achievement, or you bring your dream to life. We feel like we've "made it."

But, then, something funny happens. Something we didn't expect.

We begin to think about new milestones, new achievements—maybe we even develop a new dream to reach for.

And that's when we realize that the destination we reached was just a point along the way. Now there is a new destination. We keep moving. "There" becomes "here."

And if "there" can become "here" just like that, maybe there was never any "there" to begin with.

Get What You Want By Not Knowing What You Want (Let Go of the Specifics)

Not knowing what you want is a great place to be. But not in the general sense. I mean in the specific sense.

It's still a good idea to have some kind of direction that you are walking in. A general sense of what you desire in life. But you don't have to have all the specifics worked out, and, in fact, it may be better if you never work out all the specifics.

Because the truth is, I don't know that you could imagine every detail of what you really wanted. And if you tried, you would be limiting yourself.

Think of something you have now that you love, but that at one point in your life you couldn't imagine. Clearly, you didn't know that you wanted it, but it worked out really great.

Specifics make us feel comfortable, because we feel like we have some control over getting the things that we want, but we also get attached to specifics, and too much attachment usually doesn't lead to the results that we want.

The next time you find yourself tempted to get really specific about the things you want, hold off. Remember what you desire in the general sense, but leave out what color it is, at what time you will find it, and who will deliver it to you, because, honestly, you can never know those things. That's what makes it exciting.

The Myth of the Perfect Answer

If you are like me, and reading this blog, you are probably looking for answers.

There seem to be so many questions, and not quite enough answers. It's easy to start thinking that if you can find the perfect answer, some of the questions will start disappearing.

Seeking is a good thing. If you have an interest in self-improvement, you are always looking for new information, insights and practices that can further your personal development. But what happens when the answers you receive are never perfect? Would you pass up something that works for something that could be perfect?

When this happens, we can begin to seek for things that simply don't exist, and bypass things that are good options for us right now. Looking for perfection creates an impossible circumstance. Theory and practice are never quite on the same page, but if we do our best to see that our beliefs work as best as they can in our lives we will do alright.

It is very tempting to think that if we can just find that "one": religion, political belief system, diet/fitness program, career path, relationship etc. that we will then be whole. But, of course, then something would change in our lives and we would need a new answer.

I find myself falling into this trap periodically, and I always feel better when I start to pull myself out of it. It's funny, because when you are looking for that perfect answer you can actually feel foggier than if you are living bravely between what may be and what is. Letting go of that perfect answer is liberating.

Letting Go of the Perfect Answer

When an Answer No Longer Serves You, Change It – As our life circumstances change, the answers we need change also. In college, my fitness routine was to go to the gym 5 days a week to complete a cardio workout and lift weights. Now that I work full time and commute, that's no longer the answer for me. My current answer is to walk and practice yoga. The answers change throughout your life.

Trial and Error – Maybe the only answer we have is to try things out and see what works. What works for you the most at this point in your life?

Find Substance In The Tension – When we can't translate theory directly into practice, we simply have to work with what we are given. When you don't have exactly what you need, you have to adjust to what there actually is. And, you may just come up with a great answer. For now, anyways.

The Best You Have Is Sometimes Just OK – Sometimes the best you can do is not that great, but if it's all you've got, just go with it. Living with answers that are just satisfactory is a part of seeking. If you stick with it long enough you may find that this has encouraged your growth.

Not Everything Is Meant To Be Solved – We want to solve things. But sometimes we are given a problem that we can't seem to find a rational answer for. In that case, seeing where the problem takes us is often the answer. We usually want to lead the problem, but sometimes, let the problem lead you.

There Are No Rules

Rules make us feel comfortable.

We follow the rules, do what we are supposed to do, and reap the reward at the end.

Follow the rules, get the prize. Easy.

Only I'm not so convinced that there really are any rules.

For one, rules can be circumvented. If you can find a way around the rule, while still technically not breaking the rule, then suddenly the rule doesn't really exist.

And, rules can change (and quickly, too). Usually by someone or something powerful. And the rules that you have been following are now obsolete (along with your prize).

So what do you do when there are no rules? Break them all? Make your own? Go live by yourself on a mountain?

No. Just expect the rules will change.

You can follow them (it's always your choice anyway), just know that the rules you follow now, you might not be following ten years from now.

Rules are always a part of a context, and when the context changes so do the rules. Rules don't exist by themselves.

You might hear people say "that's the exception, not the rule" to discredit the exception. But I find myself paying closer attention to the exception.

You never know, it might be the new rule one day.

Discover Opportunities You Never Imagined; Embrace Uncertainty

Do you know what's going to happen to you tomorrow? The answer to this question is inevitably "No." Even if you have the best plans and schedules, you can't predict for sure what's going to happen.

So how do you deal with uncertainty? By accepting it.

Uncertainty Is Stressful (But It Doesn't Have To Be)

Letting uncertainty happen is stressful. It scares us when we don't know what's going to happen because we imagine all kinds of bad and undesirable things that might occur. We feel that we can't leave too much up to chance. But when we try to eliminate all uncertainty, not only do we block out the bad stuff that could happen we also block out the good things that could happen—things that we never guessed might occur.

When you make your plans too rigid you limit yourself to past experiences and those things that you can imagine happening. But what about all the things that could happen that you can't imagine? That's where you miss out. Allowing some uncertainty keeps you open to things that you never could have guessed would happen. Some of those things may not be pleasant, but some of those things are opportunities that will take you in a direction you didn't know existed.

Uncertainty Increases Possibility And Creativity

Living with uncertainty increases possibility and creativity in your life. Possibility when you are open to experiences that you never had before and creativity when you adapt to circumstances you never thought would happen. You need these things because they increase your opportunity for growth. When you have a goal that you are trying to reach you can't imagine exactly how you might get there, and when you try to plan for everything that might happen you limit your experiences.

It's usually not what's straight ahead of us that is really rewarding, it's the things we notice from the periphery. But if we are focused exclusively on what's straight ahead of us, we tend not to notice things on the side, and those are missed opportunities.

Life On Replay

We want to know what's going to happen to us because we will then know how to act, but the only things that we know are those things that have already happened to us, and essentially, when we always want the known, we live exclusively in the past. This means that our lives are simply being lived on "replay."

Besides, we can't ever really control everything even when we try to. We are adapting to circumstances constantly— whether we want to or not. So the choice is whether you will gracefully accept what comes to you or whether you will go kicking and screaming all the way.

Start Small

Begin to challenge your uncertainty threshold by spending time in an uncontrolled, unplanned-out, unstructured environment. You don't have to do it in an environment where things really matter, like at work. But the next time you have a day, or an afternoon or an hour to spare, just see what happens rather than deciding what you want and making a plan to get there. Next time you work on your hobby don't have any goals, go off and explore a new part of your city, a hiking trail, a park, or just decide to follow your whims for a certain amount of time. The point is not to try to get anywhere.

Always trying to control is a fruitless activity. It causes stress and discomfort because life has a way of doing what it wants and not what we want. Practicing uncertainty can help to alleviate the stress that you feel when you have to adapt to a circumstance that you did not plan.

The Hard Way

Sometimes you learn things the easy way. You listen to advice from someone who's more experienced than you. You read an article on "best practices" for whatever you're doing. And then you actually do those things, and it works out for you.

The information was out there. You followed it. And it worked out. Great.

But some other things you learn the hard way. You hear the advice. You read about what you're supposed to do.

And then you do something else entirely. Even if you sort of, kind of, have this feeling that it might not be the wisest choice.

And whatever it is doesn't work out. Maybe it's even a huge mess. Or what happens is downright embarrassing. But, still, it's done.

This is the hard way because now you have to take a long look at what happened, what you did and what went wrong. And now you're struggling. And maybe you're indecisive. Or maybe you know that you haven't got a clue what you're doing. But you still press on.

This is the hard way. You think back on those people who gave you advice and the articles you read and you really wish that you had done those things because then you would have taken the easy way. But you didn't. You took the hard way.

And then something happens. A breakthrough. Something goes right. You get a clue. And it feels rewarding because you struggled to get there. And now you feel like you've reached a peak. Maybe not even a peak, maybe just a hill. But still, you had to climb upwards to get there. And now you've gotten somewhere.

And once you hit that first peak, you feel like there are probably a few other peaks that you can get to and so you keep walking. And soon enough, the hard way is starting to feel like the easy way. Which is the way you should have taken from the beginning.

But you didn't. You took the hard way.

And because of that, it's now easy.

PART SIX:

CREATING

The Thing About Following Your Heart

"Follow your heart" is a piece of advice that gets thrown around a lot. And, by the way, I actually really like this advice.

But the thing is, there's something that people aren't telling you when they tell you to "follow your heart."

The thing that they're not telling you is this:

Following your heart is a dangerous journey.

Now, you may or may not wind up in actual physical danger, but I will absolutely guarantee you that you will end up in psychological danger.

What's psychological danger?

Psychological danger is when you feel pulled to do something that's socially unacceptable in some way. Psychological danger is when you have to put your pride/ego aside to do something that's calling to you. Psychological danger is when you have to actively go toward conflict and discomfort because that's the way you feel attracted. (There's probably a few more examples here, but you get the point.)

Basically, psychological danger breaks you down in some way, so that what is left over is more essentially you. But it's not fun and it's not pretty.

This is where your heart will lead you.

Now, your heart will lead you to some really cool places too. Places that don't require putting yourself in that danger, but it will absolutely take you to those places that, consciously at least, you don't really want to go.

That's why the pull of your heart is so strong. In order to get you to these places there has to be some serious energy behind that pull.

95

And this is why, many times, no matter what's coming out of their mouths, people much prefer to follow their heads. Because it seems like a much safer way to go. And it is.

It's just not nearly as rewarding.

What If You Couldn't Succeed?

Sometimes when we're stuck, the well-meaning person we're talking to might ask us, "What would you do if you couldn't fail?"

And this is a good question, as many of us are afraid of failure in our endeavors, so if we imagine a world where the possibility of failure is completely removed, this might get us moving forward in a way we hadn't thought of yet. It opens possibilities for us.

But, earlier this week, I flipped this question around, and asked myself "What would I do if I couldn't succeed?"

I imagined a world in which I somehow knew for certain that I would never succeed. Specifically, I was thinking about writing fiction and being able to support myself fully from that one day, which is a "non-goal" that I have.

I asked myself, "If I somehow knew for certain that I could never, ever succeed in writing fiction and having a full-time income come from that, what would I do? How would I go about writing/publishing? How would I live my life?" And almost immediately, I felt a sense of freedom and relief.

In a nutshell, if I knew I could never succeed with writing, I would do whatever I wanted to do. I would follow my creativity and inspiration wherever it lead. I wouldn't worry and fret about this and that not happening. I would experiment, I would take risks, I would do things because I was interested in them or because I wanted to learn more or because I simply enjoyed them.

I might not ever succeed, but I would never fully fail either.

Whereas the question "What would you do if you couldn't fail?" removes the fear of failure, the question "What would you do if you couldn't succeed?" removes the barriers to following your inspiration, taking risks, and being as creative as you can be.

Frankly, these are the same questions, just asked in a completely opposite way. Two sides to the same coin.

If I could never succeed, then I would do things that creatively excited me, even if I thought it possible that it wouldn't make a big splash with readers.

If I could never succeed, then I wouldn't worry so much about making mistakes, since they would make no difference anyway. I wouldn't worry about not having this or not having that. I would just work with what I had right now, knowing that, at least in this moment, it's enough. And that when I did need more, I would get it.

If I could never succeed, then I would take breaks and live the other parts of my life whenever I felt that I needed to, because writing/publishing wouldn't have to be this gray cloud that hung over my life all the time, mocking me because I hadn't "made it" yet. I have an entire life to live, and writing is just a part of it. It would be a shame if I could never truly enjoy my life as a whole. But, if I could never succeed, then I can fully participate and be present to all parts of my life, which is quite a gift.

For all the striving that I've done, I'm not really sure that it's gotten me anywhere, and along the way, I forgot to look out the windows and enjoy the scenery.

Because the real truth is, I might never succeed, and if that happens, I don't want to have put all my eggs into this one part of my life and have ignored/avoided everything else. Because no matter how much I enjoy writing/publishing, it's not my life, it's not who I am, it's not me. I'm me.

So, if I could never succeed, then I'm actually free to fail and be present to the process along the way. And that is all I can ask for.

I would hate to get to the end of my life and be disappointed because I didn't achieve something, as if that was the only marker for a life well lived. And let's face it folks, at the end, you're going anyway, and when you're gone, everything that you've done or didn't do, doesn't matter anymore.

But, if I'm free to fail, then I'll write that story that a lot of people might not like, because I enjoy writing it and there are at least a few people who will enjoy reading it.

If I'm free to fail, then when I'm writing the story that a lot of people might not like, and I want to write something that might not work, or that's too outrageous, or that will get criticized, I'll write it anyway, because I'm experimenting and seeing where that takes me.

If I'm free to fail, and learning something new in the publishing/promotion process, I'll just do it, even if I feel like I haven't got a clue what I'm doing. Because I can learn along the way, and change things as necessary. It's not that big of a deal.

So if you've tried asking yourself how you would live if you couldn't fail, and couldn't quite get moving the way that you would like, you might want to try asking yourself how you would live if you couldn't succeed, and see where that takes you.

I could also just be really weird. But flipping this question around has brought me a freedom that I hadn't found before, and ultimately, gives me a new lens through which to look at my life.

So if you knew, for certain, without a doubt, that no matter what you did you couldn't succeed? What would you do?

The Thing You Can't Not Do

A lot of people want to know what their life purpose is. A lot of people want to achieve something great. And, a lot of people want to find out what it is they truly love to do.

So, they go looking for that thing.

But, they have it backward. They should look at the things they already do. And more specifically, they should identify the thing they can't not do.

You probably do it everyday. But you probably don't recognize it. Because you think that everyone else does this thing too. Or, you think that you're not really doing anything.

But that's only because this thing is so natural to you it doesn't seem like you're doing anything. But you are.

About six years ago, I realized that I did something that I couldn't not do. I had been doing it for years, since I was 12 or 13 years old. But I never thought anything of it.

I realized that pretty much every day of my life, I would experience something or observe something or read something and then, no matter where I was, I would begin to think about it.

I would think about why it interested me. I would break down its parts and see how they all fit together. I would ask questions about it. I would examine all parts of it until it left me with a question, or an insight or a better understanding of why something is.

I would do this automatically, simply because I was so interested in what I had just seen. I was drawn to it. I never tried to do it, I just did it because it was something I couldn't not do.

One day, I began to write down some of these thoughts. And those thoughts later turned into blog posts and then short stories and then novels. And wouldn't you know it, all of the sudden, I was a writer.

And, to think, that for years I never even acknowledged what I was doing.

Why Do You Want To Do That?

You have probably heard this question more than once in your life.

Sometimes when we share an idea that we are excited about with others, it's met with the above question. Maybe the idea seems like it won't work, or maybe nothing like it has been done before. Maybe it seems out of character for you, or maybe it's just downright crazy. Whatever the reason, other people often respond to us with—

Why Do You Want To Do That?

Although it may be said with good intentions, this question ultimately serves one purpose—to dissuade you from doing whatever it is that you want to do. And it never feels good to be on the receiving end of it.

So, the next time that someone comes to you with a new idea, something that they are really excited about. Stop yourself from asking the above question, and say to them—

I think you should give that a try

How To Discover A Creative Activity You Love

A creative activity is any activity that brings something new into the world. What that "something new" is will be up to you.

So, how do you find a creative activity that you love to practice? That's simple. It's an activity that makes you feel excited, energetic and where you have a desire to bring something new into the world. But if that doesn't give you any clues, here are a few more tips.

Think of something you have always wanted to try. What has been nagging at you for months, or even years, to give it a try? There's a very good chance that this thing that has gripped your mind is something you would likely be good at and enjoy very much. Trust your internal guidance.

Look past the traditional "arts" if you need to. Your favorite creative activity may be something traditionally thought of as creative. But it might not. If you have no interest in painting, sculpting, writing, dancing, etc, don't worry! This doesn't mean you are not creative. It simply means you will have to be creative in finding and defining your favorite creative ability.

Think back to when you were a kid. Kids are much freer in expressing themselves and usually have no qualms about stating what they do and don't want to do. That's why when you look back at yourself as a kid, and think about what you really liked to do, you probably really liked to do it. So, what did you really enjoy doing as a kid?

Think of something you have watched someone else do and thought was cool. If you pay attention to what attracts you, you will get some really good clues about what it is that you would love to create. When was the last time you saw someone do something that you wished you could do? Maybe you should try that thing out.

Think about what you like to "play" with. Play is a huge element in being creative. Play requires the player to suspend boundaries temporarily, let go of results and expectations and try many things without (too much) fear of failure. What do you like to play with?

What "problems" do you want to solve? Solving a problem is another huge element in being creative. The problem doesn't have to be on a global level and it may not even seem like a "problem" on the surface. It may be something like, "how do I express what it feels like to watch the seasons change?" or "how do I throw an enjoyable party?" Look for the "problems" that make you want to find a solution.

Just pick something! In the end, trial and error may be the best approach. Pick an activity you think you will like and start doing it. If it holds your attention and you feel excited about it, you've probably found something. If not, and you don't feel very energetic about it, scrap it, and move onto something new. You can play around with your creative ambitions as much as you like.

What Have You Always Wanted To Try?

Can you think of something that you've always wanted to try, but haven't? What's holding you back?

The desire to do something is all you need to begin a new endeavor. You may even surprise yourself at how quickly you catch on to this new activity.

When you think about the thing that you want to try, your mind may start saying these things:

I am too busy.

I am too tired.

I might fail.

I am scared of looking foolish.

I don't know what I am doing.

It's fine to feel one or all of these things, but don't let them run your life. When your mind starts talking to you like that, leave your mind behind and go visit your center.

In your center, feel the strength of your desire, and trust that feeling. Everything has it's beginning in desire. Allow yourself to say "I want." And then go do it.

The Power To Create

When you think of the word "creative" what do you think of? Many of us automatically think about famous artists, musicians, and writers, but how often do you think of yourself when you hear that word?

Creativity is more than just paintings, songs and novels (although, certainly those things are creative). If we make creativity something that is outside of what we are capable of, we sell ourselves short.

And, it's something that happens everyday—when we solve problems, adjust to detours, simply live our daily life.

Creativity is so important to us because that's when we feel that "spark of life" that we so often miss. And while we are all creative everyday in similar ways we are also all creative in unique ways.

We often think of tangible things when we think of creativity, but you can also create non-tangibles, like organization, clarity and laughter. At a former job, I used to work with a lady who I would describe as being great at creating laughter. At a time when we had stressful deadlines and tedious assignments to do, she would tell us a story and have us practically rolling on the floor as we laughed so hard. That laughter relieved stress and put our work into proper perspective. That was her creation. Even though we couldn't touch and see it, we could feel it.

But many of us aren't creating in our life, and we feel the negative effects of that. Somewhere we may believe that creativity is "frivolous," or feel we just don't have time for it. Or we may just be afraid.

The Barriers To Creativity

Fear of Failure – Failure is necessary for creativity, because when you are creating you have to be willing to try things that you don't know will work. If you are afraid to fail, your creative efforts will always fall short, because you are not exercising all the possibilities that you think of. You cut them off before they can exist.

Fear of the Unknown – They say that what we don't know can't hurt us, but it sure scares the hell out of us! When you are creative, you don't know what might happen. Maybe what you thought you were creating changes form as you are in the process. Or the people you share it with react to it in a way that you didn't foresee. Creation is the process of bringing something into the world that has not yet existed. That process always involves letting go of the known.

Fear of Rejection – Maybe most of all, what we really fear when we are creative is being rejected. We fear that others won't understand why we need to do this, or won't like our final product. Maybe they will laugh at what we have created. Ironically enough, creativity is such a basic need of every person that we intrinsically understand the need to create, even if we are not aware of it. When we share our creations we share ourselves.

Invite Creativity Into Your Life

Start something you've always wanted to try – Have you been interested in something that you have no experience with, but think it would be really fun to try? That may just be your unique creative vision calling to you. Seek out an opportunity to try this thing, you may find something great there.

Explore with no purpose – You don't always have to have a goal when you engage in an activity. Sometimes it's best to just set out and see what happens. You can't always plan what you would like to happen, so take a step into the unknown. You can never be sure what you might find.

Rest – If you want to be more creative, get some more rest. Taking your conscious mind off of the problem you are trying to solve or off of the thing you want to create allows your subconscious mind to make connections between things you wouldn't have thought of. When you return to your creation, you will have brand new insights.

Purposely do something in a way you wouldn't normally do – We tend to get rigid with our daily routines, so if you want to look at your world more creatively, break those routines. This could be something simple like driving a different way home from work, or solving a problem backwards from the way you would normally do it. Take a chance and do something you wouldn't normally do.

See the world as possibilities – It can be easy to see the world around us as a place that has a set of rules that can't be broken. But, why can't you? At the least, changing your perspective to see that the world is not as rigid as you think opens your mind to the possibilities that exist around you. Those possibilities are where creativity lies.

Accept both success and failure as options – When you are creating, you have two options: you can succeed at what you were hoping to do or you can fail at it. Many people much prefer success, but failure is also a good option. Failure always tells us how to be a success, so decide that you will accept both of them.

Be courageous – There is always fear where there is creativity. Be courageous in bringing your creations to life.

Share it with others – What use is being creative if you don't share what you have created? We all have tremendous potential to create things that others need. When we share those things, we are contributing to our community.

Encourage others in their creativity – How many times have you been discouraged by some "well-meaning" friend or relative when you brought up something that you wanted to create? This happens all the time. We don't want to see the people we care about disappointed or struggling so we discourage them from things they want to try. Next time someone you know brings up something they want to create (even if you think it's a little crazy) tell them to give it a try.

See creativity as something that happens everyday – You are creative at home. You are creative at work. You are creative simply by living. Creativity is not out of your experience. Even when you are not engaging in your own unique form of creativity, remember that creativity becomes a part of your life as much as you want it there.

Act From Yourself

Our actions have many motivations, but the best motivation we can have is personal desire. When we act from personal desire we act from ourselves.

Here is an example. Let's say you want to be a doctor. And you want to be a doctor because you want to help people increase their level of well being. You believe that physical health and feeling good are the foundation for a fulfilling life. Within this motivation there is your own desire to do something, and a desire to contribute to others in a very specific way. In this example you are acting from your own self, from your own desire.

Let's look at this from a different perspective. You want to be a doctor. And you want to be a doctor because your Grandfather was a doctor and your parents think it would be great if you followed in his footsteps. Based on your parents' wishes, you decide to attend medical school. In this example, there is no personal desire to practice medicine, only the desire to influence how other people think and feel about you. Also notice that there is no particular desire to contribute in a certain way (even though you will help people based on the fact that you practice medicine). In this example, your actions are based on other people.

When your actions are based on others, there is no force behind them. No power. And, you have no control over how people think and feel about you anyway, so the approval you chase is always just out of your reach.

When your actions are based on yourself, your own desire propels you forward in a way that nothing else can. Obstacles and temporary failure don't upset you that much, because you know that you will find a way around them.

The Strength of Acting From Yourself

Your actions will be:

Persistent: There aren't any obstacles that will stop you, only those that will temporarily slow you down as you figure out a way around them.

Courageous: When you need to get past the gate of fear, courage is the key that unlocks it. It's difficult to be courageous consistently, but with your own desire motivating you it becomes easier to access.

Creative: When you are seeking something you desire, your creativity is in full force. That's because the road is not straight and wide, usually it's twisty, full of undergrowth and probably with a few dead trees blocking the way. You will have to be creative in getting around obstacles.

Enjoyable: This is very important and, in many ways, makes results easier to achieve. When you love the act of doing something without worry about the results, the results tend to come. When the result is all you want, it seems to get farther away.

Ensure Your Actions Are Your Own

Say "I Want": All of your actions that arise from you start with the phrase "I want." To say this without guilt or shame connects you to your personal desires and makes you want to realize them. Make a list of all the things that you want to do that would contribute to the well being of others. Make sure they are things you would love to do.

Understand You Don't Control Others' Approval: Wanting approval from others is not the problem, we all do. But sometimes you have to act in spite of it. Usually, chasing someone's approval is the very worst way to try and get it. You don't have any control over another person's thoughts and feelings about you, so trying to please others (especially at your own expense) is mostly a fruitless activity. Use courage to act on your wants, even when it feels like you may lose the approval of others.

Detach Yourself From the Result: And now, for the most difficult step. Personal desires are not only enjoyable to achieve, but they are also simply enjoyable to pursue, even when they are very challenging. There is something very fulfilling about pursuing a personal desire even if there are no guarantees that it will come true. Discover enjoyment in the process and you can let go of the result.

PART SEVEN:

FOR WRITERS

How I Write

I wanted to talk about my process for writing in this post because I feel like I go about it a little differently than many writers do.

I use my intuition a lot when I write instead of outlines, plans and notes. I really like to start fresh where I start out with not much more than an idea or a particular scene in mind. And in fact, it is often an image that I start with.

A setting with some characters and some idea of the interaction taking place between those characters will pop into my mind. And it really does seem to pop out of nowhere. I think sometimes something going on around me inspires the pop, but it happens so fast I'm not always aware of the connection.

With my novel, North, I had this image of a young woman riding in a convertible up a long highway. And it was very clear to me that she was running from something even though she also had a sense of freedom and adventure. That's what started the story for me, that one image. Granted, North kind of percolated with me for a while. So I would get other scenes in my mind from time to time or I might think about a particular character and see how they fleshed out. But it was all mental. I had no notes of any kind when I started writing that story.

And that brings me to another point. I generally write about 500 – 1000 words in a sitting, and during any particular writing session, I'm only focused on those particular words. That little section of the story. Whatever wants to come out of me at that time is what goes onto the screen. I may get little ideas about what comes after or what I think would be really cool to add into the story, but if it doesn't flow out of me when I'm writing, it doesn't go into the story.

I've had times before when I'm trying to work in an idea to a story that just won't seem to go in nicely. No matter how hard I try to add in this element that I thought would be really cool, the flow gets broken and the story stops working, and I get stuck. I've learned to never try to force an element into a story. No matter how good of an idea I thought it was, it just won't feel right in the story. Not to me and not to readers either, I suspect.

So when I'm writing it's just me and those thousand words and that's all I need to know of the story for today. The next piece will come to me tomorrow.

There's also an element of "danger" when I write this way. Not knowing how this all works out before hand, I feel like I could get lost at any moment and ruin the whole story. But I think that's where the spark comes from. That spark of life that makes a story engaging. Just like in real life I don't exactly know where I'm going. I know where I'm going today (for the most part) but that's it. It's when you piece together many days in a row that you get somewhere, but on day 1 you can't see day 50 (of course on day 50 you can see day 1 and piece together where you've been). I like that I don't know where I'm going. I think that gives the story life.

And when I'm done, I'm done. I do like to circle back through the story and read it as a whole, especially as I've been putting it together in pieces but I'm not usually making major changes to the story unless they are necessary for clarity and understanding. The story won't be perfect. They never are. But readers are forgiving of little inconsistencies here or there, a plot hole or two or maybe even something that's just a little too outrageous, even for fiction. If they're enjoying the ride, they don't mind a bump now and then.

At the end of all this, I hope that I've told a story in the way that only I could tell it. Even if that scares me a bit, because I know that both my strengths and my flaws will be in it. And I hope that I've enjoyed myself, because, well, that's a big part of why I do this.

And then it's on to the next one…

An Easy Motivation Tip For Writers

Sometimes I just don't feel like sitting down to write.

And I'm not talking about the times when I really need a break, or there's another pressing activity that really needs my attention. I'm talking about those days when my motivation is just a little off.

In order to get myself into my desk chair and in front of my laptop, I trick myself just a little by telling myself that:

I'll just sit down and write 250 words.

Usually when I sit down to write I have a goal of 1,000 words. This usually takes 45-50 minutes. So on days when my motivation is a little off I tell myself I only have to write 250 words, which will only take about 10 minutes.

It's enough to get me into my chair and get started, and the best part is that often when I hit 250, I keep going and maybe I get to 500 or 700 or even to my original goal of 1,000 words.

And if I don't, then at least I've got those 250 words, where otherwise I would have had zero.

Catching A Story

I have a specific experience of getting a story idea and then committing that story to tangible form.

And it's just my experience. For as many different writers as there are, there are just as many experiences of writing and the process of writing.

But, for me, when I get an inspired idea and begin to write that inspired idea, it's like "catching a story." Like catching it out of the air.

Lately, I've used writing prompts to start all my stories. So first there's the experience of finding, or being lead, to a story prompt.

For instance, I write a story (free) every month for my newsletter. This month when I sat down to write my story, I considered my favorite prompt sources and used my intuition to be pulled toward one of the sources.

I first checked out my Twitter Prompts list, which has been a good source for me lately, but wasn't really feeling anything there. But I was feeling drawn to a list of Erotic Story Word Prompts, even though I wasn't going to write anything erotic (this is for my newsletter after all). I figured I could pick a few off the list and write a PG-13 or below short romance story, which is what I did.

So now that I had my words/phrases for the story, I let an idea start coming to me. I didn't force this idea or try to have any kind of an agenda with it. It feels very much like receiving to me, rather than a more active crafting.

I tend to think of it like this: **The story exists somewhere in the story realm (wherever that is) and I simply spot it and allow it to tell itself to me.** Or, in other words, I catch it.

There's also a timeliness aspect to catching a story. I used to write batches of short stories for my newsletter at one time, like maybe 6 or so. Then when it came time to send one out, I had a story ready to go. But I changed this recently. Now, I'm writing the story the week before I send out a newsletter, so that the story is "fresh."

I made this change partly based on this idea I heard in blogger Steve Pavlina's Deep Abundance Integration course. I'm paraphrasing, but it goes something like this: Inspired ideas come from picking up on "signals" from other people. And when I say signals, I don't mean body language or words or anything tangible, I'm talking about signals that can only be picked up intuitively. Like, if you were to sit at your desk and "tune in" to what's needed right now with just your intuition.

But there is very much a timing aspect to this. So a signal that you get might very well be needed now or soon and if you wait too long, it gets stale. I liked this idea and thought it was interesting, hence the change in how I write newsletter stories.

Now, of course, a longer fiction project like a novel needs more time (for me it does anyway) but I find novels have their own timing rhythms.

But for today, I just wanted to share what my process is here. And also, while I was waiting for my lunch a little earlier, the phrase "Catching A Story" came to me, and I thought, "Signal?"

NaNoWriMo And The Way I Work

NaNoWriMo 2013 is over a week underway, and so far so good.

I'm a little ahead of where I need to be in terms of word count and I'm really enjoying my story! I think "pantsing" this story was definitely the way to go, as I'm constantly surprised along the way. It's a little scary too—when I start a plot point and am not sure how it's going to play out. I have to just wait until I get there and see what happens!

All of this writing over the last week has got me thinking about the way I work, because while I'm doing NaNo I have to stretch myself a bit. Some thoughts:

A Little Each Day Or A Lot Every So Often

My work style tends to be that I like to write a (relatively) small amount each day, but write almost every day. I don't get too tired this way and I always feel refreshed when I sit down the next day to write.

In contrast, although I have been writing everyday since November 1, I've been writing amounts that are larger than what I usually write.

I'm pretty comfortable writing 1000 words in a sitting, which takes me about an hour, but for NaNo I've been trying to write at least 2,000 words per day and I've had some days where I've written over 3,000.

For some writers, these amounts in a day or in one sitting aren't bad at all, but for my little plodding fingers, feels like a lot. I'm definitely more tired after writing 2,000 or 2,500 words at a time than I am writing a thousand, but if I'm going to hit 50,000 words for the month some part of my normal process has got to give, and what's giving is the amount I'm writing in a day.

The Space Between

Another reason I like to write a little each day is that it provides me with a lot of space between writing sessions.

I can write in the morning, finish up what I want to get done for the day and not have to think about it again until the next morning.

I like that gap because I feel refreshed the next time I sit down to write. And I like to think that my subconscious is working away on the story while I'm doing other things, so when I sit back down again I'm better prepared to continue telling the story than I would have been had I been slaving over it.

I've found myself wanting to get away from my story, wanting more separation from it since I'm not getting as much of a gap between writing sessions. And I'm enjoying my story! But even still, I want more space from it.

Early Birds And Night Owls

I'm definitely a morning person and this information is not new to me. No matter what I'm doing, I simply have more energy in the morning, so, if at all possible, I like to write early in the day—no later than lunch time.

Again, NaNo has forced me to go outside my comfort zone here, and what I'm finding is that I definitely can write at other times of day, it just doesn't feel as good.

And, no matter when I write or how good I feel, when I go back through and read what I've written I can't really tell the difference, so this may just be a matter of morale for me.

I feel good when I write in the morning, so when I write in the morning I feel good. And feeling good leaves me in better spirits about the story as a whole and about life in general.

It's nice to know that I can write anytime and have it be decent. It's just interesting to me that maybe writing when I have the most energy simply leaves me feeling better overall.

With Or Without Others

I think what has surprised me the most over the past eleven days is how much I enjoyed writing along side of other people, as I often think that one reason I'm drawn to writing is because I enjoy working by myself.

Last week, I attended a "write-in" with maybe fifteen or so other writers and found it really enjoyable and motivating.

I had never, not once, written in the presence of other people who were also writing, so I was pleasantly surprised. I thought I might not be able to focus as well (not to mention that it was in the evening), but I found that pretty easy.

So what I've learned about my work process so far is that I can work outside it, but there is a reason I have a preferred work process to begin with: for enjoyment.

Thinking about all the above sections, with the exception of writing with others, I would choose my way over any other way if given the choice. It's simply what I enjoy the most.

And as far as writing with others goes, this is one of the reasons why NaNoWriMo is so great. It affords you the opportunity to have camaraderie with other writers, which is saying something considering how solitary writing is.

I think this is a great addition to my work process.

Seasons of Writing

I don't actually write very much during the summers. Fiction especially. There's something within my energy that just tells me to back off, slow down, which is something I think many of us get during these warm months.

It used to make me a little nervous. I wanted to be a consistent writer, to keep my word count up. I wanted to be productive.

But my own creative/energetic rhythms got in the way, and soon I just started to go with it. Because as my word count went down, I found that I was feeling pulled toward other activities. Publishing, marketing, administrative stuff. Summers tended to be the time when I really felt like working on all these activities that were writing-related, but not writing itself.

I found myself more in learning mode rather than producing mode, and was often teaching myself something. A couple summers ago, I dove into learning Adobe InDesign, and that's been a great investment in my skills and now I'm more than proficient with it. I often play around with stuff during the summers in a way that I don't the rest of the year. Right now, I'm playing around with designing a business card for myself and that's been fun and interesting. And it's nice because I don't have any kind of deadline on it. I can sort of work on it, then let it be, then go read an article or watch a video about some element of business card design, and then work a little more on it. There's no urgency behind it. Just play and exploration.

But as summer winds down and autumn begins, I'll start to feel the writing urge. And I'll be more in producing mode. I'll be sitting down everyday to get my thousand words in, probably working on a novel, with some short stories thrown in there too. And things will stay that way through the spring. And as June rolls around again, I'll feel myself slowing down.

There's god-only-knows how many articles out there that talk about writing schedules and all the things that go along with that–motivation, hitting targets, all that good stuff. And the thing is that for as many different writers out there there's also that many ways to design a writing schedule. You experiment and you find what works for you.

I always like to go with my energetic rhythms, not against them, but it can be hard to trust! Over time, I've learned that it really is okay to follow them and everything works out in life's way—a little messy, a little sloppy, but mostly moving forward.

PART EIGHT:

EASE AND ENJOYMENT

The F-Word

Fun, of course.

How much fun do you have as a writer? Or as a human being?

Writers have a way of talking about writing that makes everything sound very tortured. Full of strife and anguish, and I guess that will always be there. For myself, included. But what about all of the fun stuff?

Like getting to hang out in your own imagination with all the worlds and characters you've got floating around up there. Or learning something new about writing or about publishing. How about getting to know other writers, either in person or online? Some people really get into doing research for their stories. I could go on, but you get the point.

The fun tends to get pushed aside by self-doubt, fear, worry, anxiety, pressure, stress, but I wonder if focusing in on the fun might lessen those other beasts we have to contend with.

I remember the first story I wrote called Their Love Could Follow Moonstones. (It's the first story in my flash fiction collection Writing on the Walls 1.)I happened upon a writing prompt, and in fact, the prompt was the title of the story, and I just went at it. It's a piece of flash fiction so it's under 1000 words. I wrote this story with a lot of enjoyment, just enjoying my imagination and the flow of the narrative arc, enjoying getting to know the characters and the little details my imagination supplied me with about them. A little while later, I was finished.

I was so pleased with my little story. Not because it was going to bring me fame and a billion dollars but just because it had been fun to write and now it was complete. I moved on to other stories.

Fast forward to last month and I'm starting to fret about what my next novel should be. I've had this idea that's been urging me to write it, but, I don't know, maybe I should write something that's in a more popular genre or would be a little easier to sell once I publish it. I've got a writing career to think about. Is this the right novel at this time?

So I did what any sane person would do. I consulted my The Secret Language of Color Cards.

I silently asked for guidance regarding my next novel and I picked a card randomly from the deck. The card I picked was White and the little message underneath it read "Lighten Up."

Message received and understood!

I think the Universe was clearly trying to tell me to stop worrying and bring a little more fun into the process, just like when I wrote that first little story. So that's what I'm going to do when I get started on this next novel in the next couple of months—focus on fun and enjoyment. I'm betting the other details will take care of themselves.

Go Easy On Yourself

I bet you are generally friendly and compassionate to the people that you meet. But, I also bet that you don't always extend that same compassion to yourself.

You probably have a tendency to be a bit harsh with yourself when you make a mistake, fail or display a fault. We all do. But it's not necessary.

If you make a mistake—go easy on yourself. You can always fix it.

If you fail at something—go easy on yourself. You can always try again.

If you have faults (of course you do!)—go easy on yourself. You have strengths too.

If you are imperfect—go easy on yourself. Everyone else is in the same boat.

When you do something wrong, remember the things you do right. Eventually, your wrongs can become rights. That's how we learn.

Revel in the joy of imperfection. Beauty is found between what things should be and what they actually are. Nature is not perfect, and yet it is.

Remember that finding yourself takes a lot of (mis)steps. Sometimes you stumble, or even trip, and sometimes your feet are steady. Both make up a journey.

Go easy on yourself. Enjoy your walk.

Make It Easy On Yourself

I had a teacher in high school who used to say that. More specifically, she would say it to me and a friend as we chatted away the last half of the class period, rather than working on the homework that she had let us get a head start on.

My teacher would often assign us homework (this was in Calculus) and then give us the last 30-45 minutes of the class to work on it, maybe even complete it if we could (our class periods were 90 minutes). So if we were lucky we'd leave class with our homework finished and nothing we needed to do that evening. You know, easy.

But, I had a friend from the basketball team in my class, and like teenagers do, we often wanted to just hang around and talk during that time we were being given to do our homework. It felt like free time and who wants to work through calculus problems in their free time?

Often in the middle of our gab sessions, our teacher would come over to redirect us back to calculus, and say, "Girls, make it easy on yourselves. Get your homework done." And, you know, sometimes we would actually do that.

I've never forgotten about this idea of making it easy on myself, mostly because there are many times when I'm making it hard on myself. For whatever reason, sometimes I bypass the easy for the hard.

When I can, I look out for ways to make it easy. Is there something that would make whatever I'm doing simpler? Is there an easier way through? Am I missing the easy way because there is something I'm attached to in the moment or something that temporarily feels good? Good questions.

The Joy Of Procrastination

Procrastination does not have a good reputation. He steals our productivity, robs us of achievement and runs off with the attainment of our goals.

So we protect ourselves from Procrastination with shields and swords and all manner of armor and weaponry. Sometimes we feel as if we are winning and feel pretty good about ourselves.

And yet, Procrastination finds a way to get around all of our protection, because, ultimately, there is an inexplicable joy to doing things we want to do when there are other things that need to be done.

But maybe we don't need to protect against Procrastination. Maybe Procrastination is our friend. He certainly is very enjoyable company.

The Thrill Of Being Pulled

The real joy of Procrastination is in allowing ourselves to be pulled towards whatever we are drawn to.

If we lift our heads up from our work for a moment and look around, something to the side may catch our eye.

A forbidden path. The road less traveled. Whatever you want to call it, adventure and uncertainty call to us as we look off into the periphery.

Too many times we see that thing that calls to us and ignore it, feeling we should instead keep walking the straight line that we are on now. That it will be faster and more efficient.

Procrastination allows us to wander off into the grass or into the trees to find things that we never knew existed. He alerts us to the possibility of joy.

The Infinite To-Do List

When our to-do lists reach a certain length we tend to tell ourselves that if we do not work solely from the to-do list certain doom will soon be upon us.

Procrastination tells us that this is not true.

When we hang out with Procrastination for a little while (or a long while as it may be) there always comes a time when he must go home. At this time we can go back to the items on our to-do lists, to wait for him until he comes knocking on our door again.

Procrastination may come and go, but the items on our to-do list will always be there for us. So it's wise to catch Procrastination when he comes around and save our to-do list for when he's not.

Getting Stuff Done

Procrastination is a fun friend, but he has a sixth sense about when we really need to get some stuff done and allows us our space to do so.

He wants to be able to pull you with him on various whims at random times of the day, but he knows that in order for this to be possible you do have to complete some of the to-do list items.

So he goes and plays with other friends, leaving you to work and be productive. Allowing you to feel good as you mark a line through those items you've completed.

Procrastination is not clingy. He wants to have fun with you, but he knows that too much of a good thing is not a good thing. And frankly, he has to work on his to-do list too.

The Joy Of Walking

Do you ever reach a point in the day when you feel like you just can't think anymore? Do you want to exercise more during the week but find it inconvenient to do so? Are you too tired and stressed to hit the gym or go running after work? If so, consider taking a walk.

Even though walking may seem slow and not painful enough to bring you any real benefits, walking is an activity that is not only beneficial, but can provide several benefits at once. Next time you need a break or some exercise, take a walk. Not everything needs to be punishment.

Walking Is Good Exercise

It's not going to put you in the same kind of shape as an Olympic athlete, but if you are someone looking for a general level of fitness and the health benefits that come along with that, walking is a great activity. For instance, if you went out for a walk on your lunch break at work and walked at a moderate pace (3 mph) on a level surface, you would burn 136 calories (for a 130 lb person). How many calories do you burn if you meant to go running, but were too tired to go?

Walking Is Convenient

One of my favorite things about walking is that it does not require me to change my clothes (if I'm walking at a light/ moderate pace). This makes it a great activity to do at work or any other time when I have a spare 15 minutes. Also, walking can be done in a lot of settings. You can walk outside around your office building, you can walk in the mall, you can walk up stairs, or you can walk to the store. Not to mention that your feet are actually a form of transportation. If you live in an area that supports it, walking to get to where you need to go kills two birds with one stone.

Walking Brings Peace Of Mind And Great Insights

If you are looking for a mental break in your daily routine, walking is peaceful and relaxing. If you are walking outside—which I highly recommend as much as possible—being around nature has a way of changing your perspective. That project that you are worried about, the one that you have no idea how to get started on, it suddenly seems much clearer to you. Walking is also used as a form of meditation. I don't know why it works, but when you are alone and moving on autopilot (hopefully you don't have to think about putting one foot in front of the other) creative thoughts and insights just seem to come to you.

Last Thoughts…

If you are a runner and you love to run and you find it beneficial, then don't stop. But, if you are a runner and you find yourself making excuses for why you can't (read: don't want to) run or you hate running to begin with or you're just looking for some peace and calm, consider walking. You can burn calories, spend time in nature, and become more mindful all at the same time while taking a break from work. No pain, all gain.

Pursue Enjoyment To Make Everything You Do Worthwhile

How many times have you done something only because you thought you were going to get something from it, and then didn't get what you thought you would? Did you feel that this was a waste of your time and energy?

Think about what you typically do on a daily basis. How many of these things do you do simply for the sake of doing them? And, how many of these things do you do only to get an external reward?

It's not a bad thing to engage in an activity only to get a reward (I mean, we all have to eat and have a place to live, right?). But, engaging in more activities that you enjoy simply for the sake of doing them will ultimately make your days that much more worthwhile. If the reward is simply the activity itself then you always get something out of it.

In his book "Creativity: Flow and the Psychology of Discovery and Invention," Mihaly Csikszentmihalyi discussed two types of activity: autotelic and exotelic. Autotelic activity is activity you do for the sheer enjoyment of the activity itself. Exotelic activity is activity you do in order to get at some external reward. Most activities in life are exotelic, rather than autotelic.

Seeking Enjoyment For Its Own Sake

How do you find activities that you enjoy simply for the sake of doing them? You might already know what they are. If that's the case, make room for them in your life, make them a priority. Especially when your days are filled with things that you have to do, taking the time to do something you love isn't just important, it's a necessity.

And what about if you're not sure what brings you joy for it's own sake. This isn't that hard. Just ask yourself—"What do I have the greatest desire to do?" Follow your desire and you are sure to find something that you are not only very good at, but love to do for its own sake.

Seeking Enjoyment In Things You Have To Do

This one is a bit more difficult, but in a way, more import-ant as there are many things you have to do, but don't enjoy doing. Think about the goals you have for your life or per-sonal qualities you possess and look at the activity from that perspective. For instance, if you hate to vacuum the floor and clean the bathroom, but you are trying to be more mindful and meditate regularly, you can do the chores mindfully and use it as a type of meditation. If you are a very competitive person and you have a repetitive task to do at work you can see how fast you can do the activity or how you can do it the best.

Connect the activity to something about yourself and it will never be a waste of action, it will always be a learning experience.

Quality Of Experience

Why is an autotelic activity preferable to an exotelic activ-ity? Simply because of the way that you feel when engaged in the activity. When Csikszentmihalyi studied people that who did things they enjoyed but did not get rewarded for them, he found that these people were motivated by the "quality of ex-perience they felt when they were involved with the activity."

People have asked many times over—What is the key to happiness? And, the answer to this question is usually the attainment of some situation, object, circumstance or goal. People often define happiness in terms of the future, but neglect their present experience.

The quality of our experiences, while we might not be directly aware of it in the moment, go a long way towards how we feel about our day, our week, our year, our life. Seeking out activities that give us a certain "quality of experience" may not be the only key to happiness, but certainly contributes to it in a way that many other things don't.

PART NINE:

REST

When Is It Time To Take A Break

Knowing when to stop is just as important as knowing when to start. Only, we're often not that good at knowing when to stop.

Breaks are necessary for us to regain perspective, be more creative and ultimately feel good about ourselves and the way life is going. Sometimes what you need is to rest.

Signs That You Need A Break

You Feel Irritated—Ever have a day when everything that happens makes you feel irritated? That usually means that what you need is to step back. It's probably not the situation itself that is making you feel short, it's probably something inside of you. For me, this is one of the first signs that it's time to take a break.

You Feel Longing—I've been sitting at work recently, feeling a strong pull to go to the beach and be outside. Granted it is summertime and the weather is warm, but this could also be a sign that it's time to take a vacation. My work is going fine, but I can't escape this feeling of wanting to be outside. When you feel strongly pulled in one direction, take some time to listen. It's probably telling you something.

You Feel No Enjoyment—Do you still get the same enjoyment from an activity that you once did? If you don't, think about taking a break from it. You may need to bring more creative ideas to the activity. In that case, take a break and let your unconscious do some "thinking" for you. When you come back, you just may find that you see things in a different light. On the other hand, this could indicate that it's time to take a permanent break. You may need to cut this from your life.

You Feel Bored—Maybe you need to inject a fresh challenge into whatever you are doing. Once you begin to feel comfortable with something, think about how you can take it further. It's OK to be comfortable for a little while, but after some time you will get bored if you don't feel challenged. Step aside for a while and think of how you can add some challenge for yourself.

You Can't Focus—When you just can't concentrate any longer, whether in a short term or a long term sense, stop whatever it is that you are doing. At this point, if you push through, your focus is only going to get worse. If you want to be more productive, take some time off. If you are feeling restless, it means you need some rest.

You Feel Tired—When you are just plain worn out, don't push yourself further. Break your routine and do something different. You are not going to feel more energetic by pushing through, but you will feel better after a break.

Short Term And Long Term Breaks

In your life, you need both short term and long term breaks. A short term break is taking a 20 minute power nap in the afternoon. A long term break is putting your blog on hold for a month, while you think about what it is that you really have to say.

Regularly taking both types of breaks is important. Both your body and mind need restorative time. You can't be all action and no inaction. Being idle is a part of being productive and fulfilled. It's hard to understand, but things happen when we are resting that we are not quite aware of. It's the maintenance we need to live our lives as we want to.

Don't wait for the above symptoms to assail you at the wrong moment. Make regular short term and long term breaks a part of your life.

Be Idle And Achieve

Idle time is one of the least valued and most valued things in our lives. Least valued because we tend to think that faster is always better and most valued because we're already going so fast that all we want is to be able to slow down. Periods of slowness are important not because of what we are doing, but because of what we are not doing.

You Need Idle Time To Examine Yourself Objectively

Without time for self reflection you can't see yourself. Self reflection is like being out of body and looking at yourself at the way another person would look at you. (Although you have an advantage because you also know your thoughts and feelings.) This is necessary in order to be able to evaluate how things are going – to decide what parts of your life should go and what needs to stay. This is a period of time that gives you the proper perspective to make decisions. Although self reflection needs vary among people, don't cut out this time with yourself all together.

Slowing Down Helps You Avoid Sloppy Mistakes

Being quick or timely is not the same thing as being rushed. We need to be able to do things quickly, and as we gain more experience doing something we are able to do things quicker, but with the same amount of quality. Rushing is speed without quality.

Have you ever rushed around your house in the morning, barely making it out of the door on time, and then realized that your keys are in your house, behind your locked door?

Great Solutions and Insights Tend To Happen When You Are Engaged In A Simple Activity

I always have great ideas in the car or when I'm doing something routine. I hear a lot of people say that they have great ideas in the shower or when they are taking a walk or doing some other form of physical activity. Giving our busy minds a rest seems to bring out the best in them.

In his book "Creativity: Flow and the Psychology of Discovery and Invention", Mihaly Csikszentmihalyi has this to say about the "Aha! Experience":

"The insight presumably occurs when a subconscious connection between ideas fits so well that it is forced to pop out into awareness, like a cork held underwater breaking out into the air after it is released."

But, in order to have a "subconscious connection" you can't be directly thinking about the problem or idea you are working on. The idea needs some room to work. You see, even when we are not doing much of anything, great things still do happen.

The Quick Guide To Daydreaming

Daydreaming…ahhh. The practice of putting your head up in the clouds when you're supposed to be keeping your feet on the ground.

We all do it. Some of us are pros, but some of us may need a little extra help with our zoning out. For those in the latter group, here are a few simple steps:

1. Choose a time and place where you are supposed to be doing something else

The number one pleasure of daydreaming is the fact that you are supposed to be doing something else while you do it. Something more practical, no doubt.

Really, daydreaming is just a very specific form of procrastination. But the benefits of daydreaming are that you don't need any equipment other than your own imagination and you can do it without anyone realizing you are doing it.

Maybe you're in a meeting, maybe you're in a classroom (possibly you're the teacher!), maybe you're listening to a boring lecture, but no matter where you are or who you're with, daydreaming is a delicious possibility.

2. Pick a subject that fascinates you endlessly

Have a favorite TV show or book that you can't get off your mind? Is there someone special you've been thinking about? Maybe you enjoy a "choose your own adventure"-type daydream. Put yourself into your dream career—spy, pop star, world leader—and go there. But only in your mind.

When your meeting is finished and you go back to your desk at your ordinary job, remember what it felt like to be on stage in front of thousands of people, rapping the latest hit song. Or how it felt to escape from the bad guys across those rooftops in a major world city. Remember when you almost fell?

Insert yourself into that TV show or book you've been thinking about. Make up a new character for yourself or embody one that you already love. How does the story change with you there?

Has your crush noticed you yet? Is that even possible? Or are they just an image you saw somewhere? Either way, form them in your mind and interact with them. That's a whole lot better than paying attention to those power point slides.

3. Come back to Earth

So, the thing about daydreaming is that you eventually do have to put your feet on the ground, or risk becoming a permanent space cadet.

Living as a powerful world leader is wonderful in your mind, but eventually you do have to live your real life and interact with the real people you know, as easy or as difficult as that may be. But keeping your feet on the ground (at least for a bit) isn't so bad, and, in fact, feels pretty good.

You've gotta have a solid foundation for all that mind travel, so you can have a platinum selling album and a real, solid life as well.

Fantasies are important because they let us know what may be possible, or what our desires are (maybe in a symbolic form), but all of us live in reality, and we must remember that.

To get your dreams into reality, you have to make them real.

Bonus Step: 4. Be careful of blurring the line between reality and fantasy

Your daydreams are your daydreams and your life is your life. Remember that.

How To Take A Nap

Recognize that you are sleepy. Or that you need a break. Maybe you'd like to feel refreshed for the second half of your day. Whatever your reasoning, acknowledge that you'd like to take a nap.

Forget About Feeling Guilty.

Let that go. If you want to rest, rest. If somewhere deep inside of you there lives a belief that says, 'adults don't sleep during the day, only four year olds do that,' let that go (and you may want to examine where that comes from—later—not during naptime, of course.) Or, if you are worried that taking a break and resting for a little bit will throw off your productivity, try it and see what happens. My prediction is that the earth won't fly off its axis and your life will be mostly the same as it was before you laid down to take a nap.

Pick The Perfect Time.

You know that time, somewhere in the middle of the afternoon, when you're dying to get horizontal and close your eyes. That's the time. For me, that sweet spot is somewhere between 2 – 4 pm (and it probably is for a lot of other people too). Going much later than 4pm for a nap, except in extenuating circumstances, leaves me feeling groggy for longer than I want. So I try to keep my napping to the mid-afternoon. You may be different. Just find your own sweet spot.

Pick The Perfect Spot.

My preferred place to nap is on the couch in my living room, with a blanket. This doesn't always work if there are other people occupying the living room, however. Sometimes I'll nap in my bed, but oddly enough, I don't prefer my bed for napping. Also, you may need to get creative if you're not at your house and you want to nap. When I'm at work, and go out for lunch, I'll sometimes see people sitting in their cars in the multi-level garage where I park with their eyes closed, presumably napping. Maybe not the most ideal spot, but it gets the job done. I do something similar except I drive to a nearby park first. It's really peaceful there and I can see green things like trees and grass. I don't always fall asleep, but that's OK. Closing my eyes in the middle of the day is luxury enough.

Set A Timer.

I used to just free-form my naps. Meaning that I laid down, fell asleep and woke up when I woke up. I might have set an alarm if I had to get up and do something, but otherwise I just let my body fall asleep and wake up when it wanted to. Now, however, I find it better to actually set a timer for napping. I'll usually set it for twenty minutes. It's amazing how refreshed I feel after being asleep for only five or ten minutes. (I don't usually fall asleep right away when I nap, and sometimes I don't actually fall asleep at all.) It might seem like five or ten minutes of sleep isn't worth anything, but I beg to differ. Sleeping too long in the afternoon will leave me groggier than I would like. I want to rest and feel refreshed, not feel like my nap is dragging behind me the rest of the day, so timing it is the way to go.

Don't Fret If You Don't Fall Asleep.

Even when I don't fall asleep, I find my naps refreshing. Just getting to be quiet, still, and comfortable while closing my eyes is fantastic. And if I do sleep, that's just icing on the cake. If you lay down and have a lot of thoughts, don't worry, when you notice you're having one, gently let it go and bring your awareness back to your body in some way. Don't turn nap time into some kind of competition or goal. Don't try to be efficient. Nap time is never wasted even if you're not sleeping.

Do It Again.

If you found your nap to be enjoyable and refreshing, do it again another day. Make it a part of your routine, even. Dare to sleep in the middle of the day. Even if only four year olds are supposed to do that.

The Art of Napping

I love to take naps. Most days, however, I'm at work and a nap just isn't possible. So when I do get the chance, I take it as often as I can.

Although napping is an art where no technique is really necessary, here are some ideas to make nap time one of your favorite pleasures.

Give Up Your Guilt—First and foremost, if you feel guilty about taking a nap in the afternoon, that will impact your enjoyment of the process. Somewhere in life we all started thinking that naps were lazy and only for children. This is false. Naps are one of my most favorite pleasures, and I predict that I am not alone. It's not that I'm being lazy, I'm simply doing something that I enjoy. And taking breaks and enjoyment are an important part of each day.

Have A Time Limit—In general, a nap-length sleep is somewhere in the 30 minute range, give or take 10 minutes. Much more than that and you may have more than a nap on your hands. I find that if I nap too long, I wake up groggy or I may not be ready to sleep that night. A nap is just a brief foray into dream-land. Keep it such and you will feel more refreshed when you do have to get up.

Pick A Place—Lucky for us, naps are not limited to just our beds. The couch, the floor, a comfy chair or outside are all good choices, but you are really not limited. In a sense, your nap-spot picks you. If you get so comfortable that you just can't help but fall asleep, that's the right place.

Pre-Nap Activity—Speaking of getting comfortable, sometimes naps become spontaneous while we've gotten sleepy reading a book or watching TV. My advice—abandon your activity that has gotten you into the nap-mood and fall asleep. There are no rules that say you have to finish whatever you were doing first!

Don't Try To Fall Asleep—If your nap is not so spontaneous and you've laid down simply for a nap's sake, don't try too hard to fall asleep. Afternoon sleepiness tends to sneak up on us, but if we try to summon it, the feeling may not come. Simply lie down and close your eyes. Even if you don't actually fall asleep, resting with your eyes clothes is enjoyable too. Usually, if you don't think about it that much, sleepiness will come.

Afternoon Light—One of my favorite parts about napping is the way the sunlight looks and feels in the afternoon. Positioning myself near a window gives me full enjoyment of the sun. It's funny because when we sleep at night, pitch black is usually optimal, but afternoon napping can make great use of the waning late day sunlight.

Don't Jump Up Right Away—When waking up from a nap, don't spring into action right away. Give yourself a few minutes to get used to the waking world again. Basking in the glow of your nap is almost as good as falling asleep initially was.

The Spider

When I was in college I studied abroad my junior year. At the university I was attending, grades for your courses were determined by one oral exam at the end of the semester. There were no other assignments and, therefore, no other grades. Your success or failure on the exam was your success or failure in the course.

During exams, I found myself in a situation where I had a couple of exams on back to back days which made studying for both a little difficult. Like many other students, I had studied a little before the exam period, but really needed to catch up in the day or two before.

I had taken an exam earlier in the day, and was already exhausted from that. Apart from the course grade resting on this one exam, it was an oral exam, which I wasn't used to. Not knowing something is one thing, but not knowing it when you are face to face with your professor trying to pass a course is another!

In the evening, I walked into the common kitchen of my building to take a short break and get a snack, dreading the upcoming night of studying and the exam I had to take first thing in the morning. It felt like my problem was engulfing me and that the universe itself had decided to sit on my shoulders. My stress levels rose as I couldn't seem to see anything but my problem ahead of me.

Then, as I stood by the window ruminating on my misery, I saw a spider. A tiny one. Just walking along the ledge of the window. For a moment, I became preoccupied with the spider, and it felt good.

I watched it move its tiny legs along the sill, just moving along, doing what spiders do. And, in that moment my "problem" seemed to regain its proper perspective and the universe had retreated from the warm spot it found on my back.

That tiny spider helped me to see that the world existed outside of me and my problem. And that everything has a proper place in the universe. Frankly, I had let my problems consume my life for a couple of days, and that's why my stress levels were rising.

I realized that just as the spider was doing nothing other than being what it was, that all I also had to do what simply be what I was. The spider neither knew nor cared about university exams, it knew only making webs, eating insects and walking along this window ledge.

In my world, being what I was, I had to take exams, but I didn't have to let that consume me any more than the spider was allowing walking along the window sill to consume him. It was simply a part of what he did.

I watched the spider for about 30 seconds, letting myself relax momentarily. And I remembered that tomorrow the exam would be over and soon after that mostly forgotten. I walked back to my room and opened my books again. But the image of that spider walking the ledge stayed with me.

7 Ways To Excel At Resting

Do you think that you get enough rest in your life? I don't just mean sleep either, although that's part of it. I simply mean downtime, time to relax and rejuvenate, time to think and just meander along.

We like schedules. We like color-coded schedules. We are great doers, but not so great resters. But, activity is most productive when followed by rest. Activity and rest go together like Night and Day—you can't have one without the other. Constantly doing from 6am to midnight is actually the same thing as laying around from 6am to midnight. How would you feel if the sun never went down? Or if it was dark all the time?

The following activities are essential for mastering the art of resting. How many of these do you excel at? Actually, don't worry about it—it's rest, right?

Eating—Technically, shoving a sandwich in your face at your desk while you answer emails is eating, as is snacking from a bag of chips while lounging on your sofa watching TV. However, truly enjoyable eating involves actually tasting your food as well as fueling your body. Not every meal has to be 5 courses and last for hours, but following a few steps will make your meals much more pleasant. Sit down (or stand, depending) at a table. Eat slower. Notice what you are tasting. Preferably, eat with other people.

Playing—Get a hobby or two, and when you spend time on your hobby, do so in a playful way. Don't make any goals— just see where the activity takes you. Or, if you have to make a goal, make it to simply explore. You'll find yourself being more creative and enjoying yourself more. Playing is not just for kids.

Napping—Find a couch or a bed or a sunny spot on the floor. Lie down. Fall asleep.

Strolling—Walking is a great way to rest. But not brisk walking, just strolling. When you stroll you notice things that you don't normally pay attention to, and the methodical movement is helpful for putting your mind at rest. Also, strolling outside brings you in contact with nature, where you can get some perspective.

Conversing—Conversation doesn't have to be about the meaning of life or any other deep philosophical topics to be pleasant and restful, just an enjoyable exchange of information and thoughts. Also, a conversation requires skillful listening as well as skillful talking. See if you can listen to what the other person is saying without thinking of what you are going to say next.

Meandering—Take some time to simply let yourself flit from one activity to another. Water the plants in your house, rearrange the book shelf a bit, play with the dog or cat for a few minutes. Move from one activity to the next without thinking much about it. Just see what catches your attention.

Sitting—Sitting is really the epitome of resting. You could sit near a window and watch whatever is outside, you could focus on your breathing (not necessarily in meditation, but that works too), but the idea of sitting is not to do anything and not even to necessarily think anything. Sometimes we can put our bodies to rest, but our minds tend to keep spinning their wheels.

Resting In The Dark

I've been slowing down the past couple of weeks. And not because I'm overly tired or exhausted. Just from a natural slowing of my work/life rhythm (Side note: I can't spell the word rhythm to save my life. Thank god for spell check.)

I haven't written any new words of fiction for a few weeks, and that's okay. I do have times of the year where my production drops off (like in the summer) and I think that's a natural part of my work rhythm.

There's stuff I could write. There always is. And, actually, I have been writing new blog posts every week for a few weeks. But the fiction I decided to let rest for a while.

Now, I'm super excited to get started working on a couple of things after the new year. But that's still a couple weeks or so away and I think it's important to go with this lower-energy feeling and take some time off right now, even though I could write/work if I wanted to.

The darkness of this time of year is making me feel quiet, still, reflective, and slow. Certain activities naturally arise from that.

Reading by the fireplace. Spending time socializing with friends and family (and of course eating and drinking). Taking a bath. Decorating. Baking. Gift buying/making/wrapping. Taking care of small things around the house. Going to the movies. Hanging out with my cat. Planning for the year ahead. Looking back on the year past.

Of course, I could work. There's no real reason not to. But I think I'll absorb the slowness of the next couple of weeks and go with it, and after that things will return to normal. And I'll feel a renewed sense of purpose and energy, like many of us do after the new year.

But for now, I'll let my brain rest. Break up my routine. Spend more time socializing. And assume that as I rest new things are being built. New connections are being made. And things are being repaired.

Being In Your Body

As a writer, I'm in my head a lot. I'm using my imagination. I'm sitting at a desk and typing on a keyboard. Let's not forget staring at a screen.

And it feels so good to get into my body. To go take a walk, or go to the gym, or head to a yoga class or even just doing some household chore that needs to get done. Being in my body brings me back to myself.

When I'm in my head, I can get pretty far away from my body. Especially when I'm in my imagination, say, writing a story. I'm living in that world for the moment. I could be miles away in some other city or country or I might not even be in this world at all. Needless to say, I need to reconnect with my body at certain intervals or I might not come back at all.

It feels good to feel my heart rate rise, or to sweat or to feel my muscles working. It feels good to be using my senses and to be focused on the sensory information I'm getting. And it just turns my mind off for a while (usually, sometimes it just won't go off) because I don't need it on all the time. I can listen to what my body is saying for a while.

Even when I'm sitting at a desk and looking at a computer screen, I can still quickly and frequently check back in with my body. Notice my breathing for a few breaths, look out the window at what's going on outside, get up and shoot a few baskets at my small basketball hoop, get up and stretch. It's really essential for staying fresh in my mind and serves to ground me in the here and now, which as a fiction writer is harder than it seems.

THE END

Create and share.

FOR INFPS

Join the For INFPs newsletter for resources, news, tips and more—all for INFPs. Newsletters come out once or twice a month and you can unsubscribe at any time. Sign up here: amandalinehan.com/for-infps-newsletter/

LEAVE A REVIEW

Thanks for reading *Productivity For INFPs*. If you enjoyed it, please consider telling your friends or posting a short review. Word of mouth is an author's best friend and much appreciated. Thanks again!

— Amanda ü

ALSO BY AMANDA LINEHAN

Young Adult Novels

UNCOVER
THE TEST
LAKESIDE

Adult Novels

NORTH
BORED TO DEATH

Short Stories

GHOST COACH
FATHER MCMAHON'S CONFESSION
EXECUTION DAY
BEN JACKSON
THE NOTE
HAIL MARY
WRITING ON THE WALLS 1
WRITING ON THE WALLS 2

ABOUT THE AUTHOR

Amanda Linehan is a fiction writer, indie author and INFP. She has published five novels, six short stories and two short story collections. Her stories have been read by readers in 86 countries. Amanda has been self publishing since 2012. Her short fiction has been published in Every Day Fiction and in the Beach Life anthology published by Cat & Mouse Press. She lives in Maryland, likes to be outside and writes with her cat sleeping on the floor beside her desk. Contact Amanda by email: amanda@amandalinehan.com, on Twitter: @amandalinehan or on her website: www.amandalinehan.com.

Printed in Great Britain
by Amazon